PENGUIN P

KU-680-280

A MIDSUMMER NIGHT'S DREAM
BY WILLIAM SHAKESPEARE

PENGUIN POPULAR CLASSICS

A MIDSUMMER NIGHT'S DREAM

WILLIAM SHAKESPEARE

PENGUIN BOOKS

PENGUIN BOOKS

Published by the Penguin Group
Penguin Books Ltd, 27 Wrights Lane, London w8 5TZ, England
Penguin Putnam Inc., 375 Hudson Street, New York, New York 10014, USA
Penguin Books Australia Ltd, Ringwood, Victoria, Australia
Penguin Books Canada Ltd, 10 Alcorn Avenue, Toronto, Ontario, Canada M4V 3B2
Penguin Books (NZ) Ltd, Private Bag 102902, NSMC, Auckland, New Zealand

Penguin Books Ltd, Registered Offices: Harmondsworth, Middlesex, England

Published in Penguin Popular Classics 1994
7 9 10 8 6

Editorial matter copyright 1937 by the Estate of G. B. Harrison

Printed in England by Cox & Wyman Ltd, Reading, Berkshire

CONTENTS

THE WORKS OF SHAKESPEARE

APPROXIMATE DATE	PLAYS	FIRST PRINTED
Before 1594	HENRY VI three parts	Folio 1623
	RICHARD III	1597
	TITUS ANDRONICUS	1594
	LOVE'S LABOUR'S LOST	1598
	THE TWO GENTLEMEN OF VERONA	Folio
	THE COMEDY OF ERRORS	Folio
	THE TAMING OF THE SHREW	Folio
1594–1597	ROMEO AND JULIET (pirated 1597)	1599
	A MIDSUMMER NIGHT'S DREAM	1600
	RICHARD II	1597
	KING JOHN	Folio
	THE MERCHANT OF VENICE	1600
1597–1600	HENRY IV part i	1598
	HENRY IV part ii	1600
	HENRY V (pirated 1600)	Folio
	MUCH ADO ABOUT NOTHING	1600
	MERRY WIVES OF WINDSOR (pirated 1602)	Folio
	AS YOU LIKE IT	Folio
	JULIUS CAESAR	Folio
	TROYLUS AND CRESSIDA	1609
1601–1608	HAMLET (pirated 1603)	1604
	TWELFTH NIGHT	Folio
	MEASURE FOR MEASURE	Folio
	ALL'S WELL THAT ENDS WELL	Folio
	OTHELLO	1622
	LEAR	1608
	MACBETH	Folio
	TIMON OF ATHENS	Folio
	ANTONY AND CLEOPATRA	Folio
	CORIOLANUS	Folio
After 1608	PERICLES (omitted from the Folio)	1609
	CYMBELINE	Folio
	THE WINTER'S TALE	Folio
	THE TEMPEST	Folio
	HENRY VIII	Folio

POEMS

DATES UNKNOWN	VENUS AND ADONIS	1593
	THE RAPE OF LUCRECE	1594
	SONNETS / A LOVER'S COMPLAINT	1609
	THE PHOENIX AND THE TURTLE	1601

WILLIAM SHAKESPEARE

William Shakespeare was born at Stratford upon Avon in April, 1564. He was the third child, and eldest son, of John Shakespeare and Mary Arden. His father was one of the most prosperous men of Stratford who held in turn the chief offices in the town. His mother was of gentle birth, the daughter of Robert Arden of Wilmcote. In December, 1582, Shakespeare married Ann Hathaway, daughter of a farmer of Shottery, near Stratford; their first child Susanna was baptized on May 6, 1583, and twins, Hamnet and Judith, on February 22, 1585. Little is known of Shakespeare's early life; but it is unlikely that a writer who dramatized such an incomparable range and variety of human kinds and experiences should have spent his early manhood entirely in placid pursuits in a country town. There is one tradition, not universally accepted, that he fled from Stratford because he was in trouble for deer stealing, and had fallen foul of Sir Thomas Lucy, the local magnate; another that he was for some time a schoolmaster.

From 1592 onwards the records are much fuller. In March, 1592, the Lord Strange's players produced a new play at the Rose Theatre called *Harry the Sixth*, which was very successful, and was probably the *First Part of Henry VI*. In the autumn of 1592 Robert Greene, the best known of the professional writers, as he was dying wrote a letter to three fellow writers in which he warned them against the ingratitude of players in general, and in particular against an 'upstart crow' who 'supposes he is as much able to bombast out a blank verse as the best of you: and being an ab-solute Johannes Factotum is in his own conceit the only

Shake-scene in a country.' This is the first reference to Shakespeare, and the whole passage suggests that Shakespeare had become suddenly famous as a playwright. At this time Shakespeare was brought into touch with Edward Alleyne the great tragedian, and Christopher Marlowe, whose thundering parts of Tamburlaine, the Jew of Malta, and Dr Faustus Alleyne was acting, as well as Hieronimo, the hero of Kyd's *Spanish Tragedy*, the most famous of all Elizabethan plays.

In April, 1593, Shakespeare published his poem *Venus and Adonis*, which was dedicated to the young Earl of Southampton: it was a great and lasting success, and was reprinted nine times in the next few years. In May, 1594, his second poem, *The Rape of Lucrece*, was also dedicated to Southampton.

There was little playing in 1593, for the theatres were shut during a severe outbreak of the plague; but in the autumn of 1594, when the plague ceased, the playing companies were reorganized, and Shakespeare became a sharer in the Lord Chamberlain's company who went to play in the Theatre in Shoreditch. During these months Marlowe and Kyd had died. Shakespeare was thus for a time without a rival. He had already written the three parts of *Henry VI, Richard III, Titus Andronicus, The Two Gentlemen of Verona, Love's Labour's Lost, The Comedy of Errors*, and *The Taming of the Shrew*. Soon afterwards he wrote the first of his greater plays – *Romeo and Juliet* – and he followed this success in the next three years with *A Midsummer Night's Dream, Richard II*, and *The Merchant of Venice*. The two parts of *Henry IV*, introducing Falstaff, the most popular of all his comic characters, were written in 1597–8.

The company left the Theatre in 1597 owing to disputes over a renewal of the ground lease, and went to play at the

Curtain in the same neighbourhood. The disputes contin-
ued throughout 1598, and at Christmas the players settled
the matter by demolishing the old Theatre and re-erecting
a new playhouse on the South bank of the Thames, near
Southwark Cathedral. This playhouse was named the
Globe. The expenses of the new building were shared by
the chief members of the Company, including Shakespeare,
who was now a man of some means. In 1596 he had bought
New Place, a large house in the centre of Stratford, for £60,
and through his father purchased a coat-of-arms from the
Heralds, which was the official recognition that he and his
family were gentlefolk.

By the summer of 1598 Shakespeare was recognized as
the greatest of English dramatists. Booksellers were printing his more popular plays, at times even in pirated or stolen
versions, and he received a remarkable tribute from a young
writer named Francis Meres, in his book *Palladis Tamia*. In
a long catalogue of English authors Meres gave Shakespeare
more prominence than any other writer, and mentioned by
name twelve of his plays.

Shortly before the Globe was opened, Shakespeare had
completed the cycle of plays dealing with the whole story
of the Wars of the Roses with *Henry V*. It was followed by
As You Like it, and *Julius Caesar,* the first of the maturer
tragedies. In the next three years he wrote *Troylus and
Cressida, The Merry Wives of Windsor, Hamlet,* and *Twelfth
Night*.

On March 24, 1603, Queen Elizabeth died. The company
had often performed before her, but they found her suc-
cessor a far more enthusiastic patron. One of the first acts
of King James was to take over the company and to pro-
mote them to be his own servants so that henceforward
they were known as the King's Men. They acted now very

frequently at Court, and prospered accordingly. In the early years of the reign Shakespeare wrote the more sombre comedies, *All's Well that Ends Well,* and *Measure for Measure,* which were followed by *Othello, Macbeth,* and *King Lear.* Then he returned to Roman themes with *Antony and Cleopatra,* and *Coriolanus.*

Since 1601 Shakespeare had been writing less, and there were now a number of rival dramatists who were introducing new styles of drama, particularly Ben Jonson (whose first successful comedy, *Every Man in his Humour,* was acted by Shakespeare's company in 1598), Chapman, Dekker, Marston, and Beaumont and Fletcher who began to write in 1607. In 1608 the King's Men acquired a second playhouse, an indoor private theatre in the fashionable quarter of the Blackfriars. At private theatres, plays were performed indoors; the prices charged were higher than in the public playhouses, and the audience consequently was more select. Shakespeare seems to have retired from the stage about this time: his name does not occur in the various lists of players after 1607. Henceforward he lived for the most part at Stratford, where he was regarded as one of the most important citizens. He still wrote a few plays, and he tried his hand at the new form of tragi-comedy – a play with tragic incidents but a happy ending – which Beaumont and Fletcher had popularized. He wrote four of these – *Pericles, Cymbeline, The Winter's Tale,* and *The Tempest,* which was acted at Court in 1611. For the last four years of his life he lived in retirement. His son Hamnet had died in 1596: his two daughters were now married. Shakespeare died at Stratford upon Avon on April 23, 1616, and was buried in the chancel of the church, before the high altar. Shortly afterwards a memorial which still exists, with a portrait bust, was set up on the North wall. His wife survived him.

When Shakespeare died fourteen of his plays had been separately published in Quarto booklets. In 1623 his surviving fellow actors, John Heming and Henry Condell, with the co-operation of a number of printers, published a collected edition of thirty-six plays in one Folio volume, with an engraved portrait, memorial verses by Ben Jonson and others, and an Epistle to the Reader in which Heming and Condell make the interesting note that Shakespeare's 'hand and mind went together, and what he thought, he uttered with that easiness that we have scarce received from him a blot in his papers'.

The plays as printed in the Quartos or the Folio differ considerably from the usual modern text. They are often not divided into scenes, and sometimes not even into acts. Nor are there place-headings at the beginning of each scene, because in the Elizabethan theatre there was no scenery. They are carelessly printed and the spelling is erratic.

THE ELIZABETHAN THEATRE

Although plays of one sort and another had been acted for many generations, no permanent playhouse was erected in England until 1576. In the 1570's the Lord Mayor and Aldermen of the City of London and the players were constantly at variance. As a result James Burbage, then the leader of the great Earl of Leicester's players, decided that he would erect a playhouse outside the jurisdiction of the Lord Mayor, where the players would no longer be hindered by the authorities. Accordingly in 1576 he built the Theatre in Shoreditch, at that time a suburb of London. The experiment was successful, and by 1592 there were two more playhouses in London, the Curtain (also in Shoreditch), and the Rose on the south bank of the river, near Southwark Cathedral.

Elizabethan players were accustomed to act on a variety of stages; in the great hall of a nobleman's house, or one of the Queen's palaces, in town halls and in yards, as well as their own theatre.

The public playhouse for which most of Shakespeare's plays were written was a small and intimate affair. The outside measurement of the Fortune Theatre, which was built in 1600 to rival the new Globe, was but eighty feet square. Playhouses were usually circular or octagonal, with three tiers of galleries looking down upon the yard or pit, which was open to the sky. The stage jutted out into the yard so that the actors came forward into the midst of their audience.

Over the stage there was a roof, and on either side doors by which the characters entered or disappeared. Over the back of the stage ran a gallery or upper stage which was used whenever an upper scene was needed, as when Romeo climbs up to Juliet's bedroom, or the citizens of Angiers address King John from the walls. The space beneath this upper stage was known as the tiring house; it was concealed from the audience by a curtain which would be drawn back to reveal an inner stage, for such scenes as the witches' cave in *Macbeth,* Prospero's cell, or Juliet's tomb.

There was no general curtain concealing the whole stage, so that all scenes on the main stage began with an entrance and ended with an exit. Thus in tragedies the dead must be carried away. There was no scenery, and therefore no limit to the number of scenes, for a scene came to an end when the characters left the stage. When it was necessary for the exact locality of a scene to be known, then Shakespeare

THE GLOBE THEATRE

Wood-engraving by R. J. Beedham after a reconstruction by J. C. Adams

indicated it in the dialogue; otherwise a simple property or a garment was sufficient; a chair or stool showed an indoor scene, a man wearing riding boots was a messenger, a king wearing armour was on the battlefield, or the like. Such simplicity was on the whole an advantage; the spectator was not distracted by the setting and Shakespeare was able to use as many scenes as he wished. The action passed by very quickly: a play of 2500 lines of verse could be acted in two hours. Moreover, since the actor was so close to his audience, the slightest subtlety of voice and gesture was easily appreciated.

The company was a 'Fellowship of Players', who were all partners and sharers. There were usually ten to fifteen full members, with three or four boys, and some paid servants. Shakespeare had therefore to write for his team. The chief actor in the company was Richard Burbage, who first distinguished himself as Richard III; for him Shakespeare wrote his great tragic parts. An important member of the company was the clown or low comedian. From 1594 to 1600 the company's clown was Will Kemp; he was succeeded by Robert Armin. No women were allowed to appear on the stage, and all women's parts were taken by boys.

A MIDSUMMER NIGHT'S DREAM

A Midsummer Night's Dream was probably written between
the autumn of 1594 and the spring of 1595. It is first mentioned in 1598, but two passages in the play itself refer to
events of 1594. The first is Titania's speech on the foul
weather (p. 35, l. 11); the summer of 1594 was more
notably wet and boisterous than 'the agedst man of our
land is able to recount'. The second is Bottom's remark
that 'to bring in (God shield us) a Lion among Ladies is a
most dreadful thing. For there is not a more fearful wild
fowl than your Lion living' (p. 47, l. 13): which would have
raised titters from the courtiers who had attended the bap-
tism of Prince Henry of Scotland on 30th August, 1594.
These and other events glanced at in the play are recorded
in the notes.

There was no one source from which Shakespeare took
the story. Some incidents he adapted from his own plays.
In *Love's Labour's Lost* he had made fun of amateur theat-
ricals as presented by the worthies attached to a great
house; in *Romeo and Juliet* Mercutio was given a long
speech on the pranks played by fairies; whilst the entangle-
ments caused when the love affairs of two pairs of lovers go
awry was the theme of *Two Gentlemen of Verona;* in that
play, too, all the lovers run to the woods.

The opening scene of the Dream is reminiscent of the
first of Chaucer's *Canterbury Tales*:

> Whilom, as oldë stories tellen us,
> There was a duke that hightë Thesëus;
> Of Athenes he was lord and governor,

And in his time such a conqueror,
That greater was there none under the sun.
Full many a richë country had he won;
That with his wisdom and his chivalry
He conquered all the regne of Femeny,
That whilom was y-clepëd Scithia;
And weddedë the queen Ypolita,
And brought her home with him in his country
With muchel glory and great solemnity.

Other details of the story of Theseus he noted from his Life in North's translation of Plutarch's Lives.

The presence of the fairies on Theseus' wedding night was perhaps suggested by Spenser's *Epithalamium,* which came out in the first weeks of 1595. Spenser, however, regarded the Puck as a malignant creature:

Ne let the Pouke, nor other evil sprights,
Ne let mischievous witches with their charms,
Ne let hob Goblins, names whose sense we see not,
Fray us with things that be not.

The play is indeed so full of wedding rites that most critics agree that it was written for some particular wedding. The only Court wedding recorded in 1594-5 was that of William, Earl of Derby, to the Lady Elizabeth Vere, grand-daughter of Lord Burghley; but no details of the festivities remain.

It is probable that *A Midsummer Night's Dream* was revised in parts. Dr Dover Wilson, in his edition, notes that in the first 184 lines of Act V the printer of the Quarto made mistakes in the line divisions of some of the verse, and further that these mistakes occur in passages written in a freer rhythm than the rest, e.g. he printed the passage on p.78, l. 3, as:

> The Poet's eye, in a fine frenzy, rolling, doth glance
> From heaven to earth, from earth to heaven. And as
> Imagination bodies forth the forms of things
> Unknown: the Poet's pen turns them to shapes,
> And gives to airy nothing, a local habitation,
> And a name. Such tricks hath strong imagination.

Dr Dover Wilson's brilliant guess is that these passages were later additions, and 'written on the margin of the MS., in such space as could be found, they presented a problem in line-arrangement which the compositor was quite unable to solve'.

A Midsummer Night's Dream was first published in 1600. It was entered in the Stationers' Register on 8th October, 1600, as 'A Book called a Midsummer Night's Dream', and soon after printed with the title '*A Midsommer nights dreame. As it hath beene sundry times publickely acted, by the Right honourable, the Lord Chamberlaine his servants. Written by William Shakespeare. Imprinted at London, for Thomas Fisher, and are to be soulde at his shoppe, at the Signe of the White Hart, in Fleet streete.* 1600'.

The First Quarto was reprinted in 1619 when William Jaggard, the printer, issued a number of Shakespearian Quartos in one volume. As he did not wish to get into trouble for printing plays which belonged to other printers he deliberately misdated the title 1600. When the play was reprinted in its place in the First Folio of 1623 a copy of the 1619 Quarto was used. It had been revised in the playhouse. Some new stage directions were added, and the punctuation of the Quarto, which was peppered with an excess of commas, was, on the whole, very carefully revised, but several new misprints were made.

A modern editor has thus the First Quarto which gives the best text, and the First Folio which gives the best punctuation. In the present edition spellings have been modernized. The text follows the Quarto, and the punctuation the Folio, except where either seemed obviously wrong. It may in some ways appear unfamiliar to those used to the 'accepted' text, but it reproduces as closely as possible the text used in Shakespeare's own playhouse.

A Midsummer Night's Dream

THE ACTORS' NAMES

THESEUS, Duke of Athens
EGEUS, father to Hermia
LYSANDER
DEMETRIUS } in love with Hermia
PHILOSTRATE, Master of the Revels to Theseus
QUINCE, a carpenter
SNUG, a joiner
BOTTOM, a weaver
FLUTE, a bellows-mender
SNOUT, a tinker
STARVELING, a tailor
HIPPOLYTA, Queen of the Amazons, betrothed to Theseus
HERMIA, daughter to Egeus, in love with Lysander
HELENA, in love with Demetrius
OBERON, King of the Fairies
TITANIA, Queen of the Fairies
PUCK, or Robin Goodfellow
PEASEBLOSSOM
COBWEB
MOTH } fairies
MUSTARDSEED

I.1

Enter Theseus, Hippolyta, with others.

THESEUS: Now fair Hippolyta, our nuptial hour
　　Draws on apace: four happy days bring in
　　Another moon: but oh, methinks, how slow
　　This old Moon wanes; she lingers my desires
　　Like to a step-dame, or a dowager,
　　Long withering out a young man's revenue.

HIPPOLYTA: Four days will quickly steep themselves in
　　　night:
　　Four nights will quickly dream away the time:
　　And then the Moon, like to a silver bow,
　　New bent in heaven, shall behold the night
　　Of our solemnities.

THESEUS: Go Philostrate,
　　Stir up the Athenian youth to merriments,
　　Awake the pert and nimble spirit of mirth,
　　Turn melancholy forth to funerals:
　　The pale companion is not for our pomp.

　　　　　　　Exit Philostrate.

　　Hippolyta, I woo'd thee with my sword,
　　And won thy love, doing thee injuries:
　　But I will wed thee in another key,
　　With pomp, with triumph, and with revelling.

Enter Egeus and his daughter Hermia, Lysander, and Demetrius.

EGEUS: Happy be Theseus, our renowned Duke.

THESEUS: Thanks good Egeus: what's the news with thee?

EGEUS: Full of vexation, come I, with complaint
　　Against my child, my daughter Hermia.

　　　　　　　Stand forth Demetrius.

My noble Lord,
This man hath my consent to marry her.
                    Stand forth Lysander.
And my gracious Duke,
This man hath bewitch'd the bosom of my child:
Thou, thou Lysander, thou hast given her rhymes,
And interchang'd love-tokens with my child:
Thou hast by moonlight at her window sung,
With feigning voice, verses of feigning love,
And stolen the impression of her fantasy,
With bracelets of thy hair, rings, gawds, conceits,
Knacks, trifles, nosegays, sweetmeats (messengers
Of strong prevailment in unharden'd youth)
With cunning hast thou filch'd my daughter's heart,
Turn'd her obedience (which is due to me)
To stubborn harshness. And my gracious Duke,
Be it so she will not here before your Grace,
Consent to marry with Demetrius,
I beg the ancient privilege of Athens;
As she is mine, I may dispose of her;
Which shall be either to this gentleman,
Or to her death, according to our Law,
Immediately provided in that case.

THESEUS: What say you Hermia? be advis'd fair maid.
To you your father should be as a god;
One that compos'd your beauties; yea and one
To whom you are but as a form in wax
By him imprinted: and within his power,
To leave the figure, or disfigure it:
Demetrius is a worthy gentleman.

HERMIA: So is Lysander.

THESEUS: In himself he is.
But in this kind, wanting your father's voice,

The other must be held the worthier.

HERMIA: I would my father look'd but with my eyes.

THESEUS: Rather your eyes must with his judgement look.

HERMIA: I do entreat your Grace to pardon me:
    I know not by what power I am made bold,
    Nor how it may concern my modesty
    In such a presence here to plead my thoughts:
    But I beseech your Grace, that I may know
    The worst that may befall me in this case,
    If I refuse to wed Demetrius.

THESEUS: Either to die the death, or to abjure
    For ever the society of men.
    Therefore fair Hermia question your desires,
    Know of your youth, examine well your blood,
    Whether (if you yield not to your father's choice)
    You can endure the livery of a nun,
    For aye to be in shady cloister mew'd,
    To live a barren sister all your life,
    Chanting faint hymns to the cold fruitless Moon.
    Thrice blessed they that master so their blood,
    To undergo such maiden pilgrimage,
    But earthlier happy is the rose distill'd,
    Than that which withering on the virgin thorn,
    Grows, lives, and dies, in single blessedness.

HERMIA: So will I grow, so live, so die my Lord,
    Ere I will yield my virgin patent up
    Unto his lordship, whose unwished yoke,
    My soul consents not to give sovereignty.

THESEUS: Take time to pause, and by the next new Moon
    The sealing-day betwixt my love and me,
    For everlasting bond of fellowship:
    Upon that day either prepare to die,
    For disobedience to your father's will,

Or else to wed Demetrius as he would,
Or on Diana's altar to protest
For aye, austerity, and single life.
DEMETRIUS: Relent sweet Hermia, and Lysander, yield
Thy crazed title to my certain right.
LYSANDER: You have her father's love, Demetrius:
Let me have Hermia's: do you marry him.
EGEUS: Scornful Lysander, true, he hath my love;
And what is mine my love shall render him.
And she is mine, and all my right of her,
I do estate unto Demetrius.
LYSANDER: I am my Lord, as well deriv'd as he,
As well possess'd: my love is more than his:
My fortunes every way as fairly rank'd
(If not with vantage) as Demetrius':
And (which is more than all these boasts can be)
I am belov'd of beauteous Hermia.
Why should not I then prosecute my right?
Demetrius, I'll avouch it to his head,
Made love to Nedar's daughter, Helena,
And won her soul: and she (sweet Lady) dotes,
Devoutly dotes, dotes in idolatry,
Upon this spotted and inconstant man.
THESEUS: I must confess, that I have heard so much,
And with Demetrius thought to have spoke thereof:
But being over-full of self-affairs,
My mind did lose it. But Demetrius come,
And come Egeus, you shall go with me:
I have some private schooling for you both.
For you fair Hermia, look you arm yourself,
To fit your fancies to your father's will;
Or else the Law of Athens yields you up
(Which by no means we may extenuate)

To death, or to a vow of single life.
Come my Hippolyta, what cheer my love?
Demetrius and Egeus go along:
I must employ you in some business
Against our nuptial, and confer with you
Of something nearly that concerns yourselves.
EGEUS: With duty and desire we follow you.

         Exeunt. Manet Lysander and Hermia.

LYSANDER: How now my love? Why is your cheek so
    pale?
How chance the roses there do fade so fast?
HERMIA: Belike for want of rain, which I could well
    Beteem them, from the tempest of my eyes.
LYSANDER: Ay me: for aught that I could ever read,
    Could ever hear by tale or history,
    The course of true love never did run smooth,
    But either it was different in blood:
HERMIA: O cross! too high to be enthrall'd to low.
LYSANDER: Or else misgraffed, in respect of years:
HERMIA: O spite! too old to be engag'd to young.
LYSANDER: Or else it stood upon the choice of friends.
HERMIA: O hell! to choose love by another's eyes.
LYSANDER: Or if there were a sympathy in choice,
    War, death, or sickness, did lay siege to it;
    Making it momentary, as a sound:
    Swift as a shadow, short as any dream,
    Brief as the lightning in the collied night,
    That (in a spleen) unfolds both heaven and earth;
    And ere a man hath power to say, Behold,
    The jaws of darkness do devour it up:
    So quick bright things come to confusion.
HERMIA: If then true lovers have been ever cross'd,
    It stands as an edict in destiny:

Then let us teach our trial patience,
Because it is a customary cross,
As due to love, as thoughts, and dreams, and sighs,
Wishes and tears; poor fancy's followers.

LYSANDER: A good persuasion; therefore hear me
　Hermia:
I have a widow aunt, a dowager,
Of great revenue, and she hath no child:
From Athens is her house remote seven leagues,
And she respects me, as her only son:
There gentle Hermia, may I marry thee,
And to that place, the sharp Athenian Law
Cannot pursue us. If thou lov'st me, then
Steal forth thy father's house to-morrow night:
And in the wood, a league without the town
(Where I did meet thee once with Helena,
To do observance to a morn of May)
There will I stay for thee.

HERMIA: My good Lysander,
I swear to thee, by Cupid's strongest bow,
By his best arrow with the golden head,
By the simplicity of Venus' doves,
By that which knitteth souls, and prospers loves,
And by that fire which burn'd the Carthage Queen,
When the false Troyan under sail was seen,
By all the vows that ever men have broke,
(In number more than ever women spoke)
In that same place thou hast appointed me,
To-morrow truly will I meet with thee.

LYSANDER: Keep promise love: look here comes Helena.

Enter Helena.

HERMIA: God speed fair Helena, whither away?
HELENA: Call you me fair? that fair again unsay,

Demetrius loves your fair: O happy fair!
Your eyes are lode-stars, and your tongue's sweet air
More tuneable than lark to shepherd's ear,
When wheat is green, when hawthorn buds appear.
Sickness is catching: O were favour so,
Your words I catch, fair Hermia ere I go,
My ear should catch your voice, my eye, your eye,
My tongue should catch your tongue's sweet melody.
Were the world mine, Demetrius being bated,
The rest I'ld give to be to you translated.
O teach me how you look, and with what art
You sway the motion of Demetrius' heart.

HERMIA: I frown upon him, yet he loves me still.

HELENA: O that your frowns would teach my smiles such
skill.

HERMIA: I give him curses, yet he gives me love.

HELENA: O that my prayers could such affection move.

HERMIA: The more I hate, the more he follows me.

HELENA: The more I love, the more he hateth me.

HERMIA: His folly Helena is no fault of mine.

HELENA: None but your beauty, would that fault were
mine.

HERMIA: Take comfort: he no more shall see my face:
Lysander and myself will fly this place.
Before the time I did Lysander see,
Seem'd Athens as a paradise to me.
O then, what graces in my love do dwell,
That he hath turn'd a heaven unto a hell.

LYSANDER: Helen, to you our minds we will unfold:
Tomorrow night, when Phoebe doth behold
Her silver visage, in the watery glass,
Decking with liquid pearl, the bladed grass
A time that lovers' flights doth still conceal

Through Athens' gates, have we devis'd to steal.

HERMIA: And in the wood, where often you and I,
Upon faint primrose-beds, were wont to lie,
Emptying our bosoms, of their counsel sweet:
There my Lysander, and myself shall meet,
And thence from Athens turn away our eyes
To seek new friends and stranger companies.
Farewell, sweet playfellow, pray thou for us,
And good luck grant thee thy Demetrius.
Keep word Lysander, we must starve our sight,
From lovers' food, till morrow deep midnight.

Exit Hermia.

LYSANDER: I will my Hermia. Helena adieu,
As you on him, Demetrius dote on you.

Exit Lysander.

HELENA: How happy some, o'er other some can be!
Through Athens I am thought as fair as she.
But what of that? Demetrius thinks not so:
He will not know, what all but he do know.
And as he errs, doting on Hermia's eyes;
So I, admiring of his qualities:
Things base and vile, holding no quantity,
Love can transpose to form and dignity.
Love looks not with the eyes, but with the mind,
And therefore is wing'd Cupid painted blind.
Nor hath Love's mind of any judgement taste:
Wings and no eyes, figure unheedy haste.
And therefore is Love said to be a child,
Because in choice he is so oft beguil'd.
As waggish boys in game themselves forswear;
So the boy Love is perjur'd everywhere.
For ere Demetrius look'd on Hermia's eyne,
He hail'd down oaths that he was only mine.

And when this hail some heat from Hermia felt,
So he dissolv'd, and showers of oaths did melt.
I will go tell him of fair Hermia's flight:
Then to the wood will he, tomorrow night
Pursue her; and for this intelligence,
If I have thanks, it is a dear expense:
But herein mean I to enrich my pain,
To have his sight thither, and back again.

Exit.

I.2

Enter Quince the carpenter, Snug the joiner, Bottom the weaver,
Flute the bellows-mender, Snout the tinker, and
Starveling the tailor.

QUINCE: Is all our company here?

BOTTOM: You were best to call them generally, man by man, according to the scrip.

QUINCE: Here is the scroll of every man's name, which is thought fit through all Athens, to play in our Interlude before the Duke and the Duchess, on his wedding-day at night.

BOTTOM: First, good Peter Quince, say what the play treats on: then read the names of the actors: and so grow to a point.

QUINCE: Marry our play is the most lamentable comedy, and most cruel death of Pyramus and Thisby.

BOTTOM: A very good piece of work I assure you, and a merry. Now good Peter Quince, call forth your actors by the scroll. Masters spread yourselves.

QUINCE: Answer as I call you. Nick Bottom the weaver.

BOTTOM: Ready; name what part I am for, and proceed.

QUINCE: You Nick Bottom are set down for Pyramus.

BOTTOM: What is Pyramus, a lover, or a tyrant?

QUINCE: A lover that kills himself most gallant for love.

BOTTOM: That will ask some tears in the true performing of it: if I do it, let the audience look to their eyes: I will move storms; I will condole in some measure. To the rest; yet my chief humour is for a tyrant. I could play Ercles rarely, or a part to tear a cat in, to make all split the raging rocks; and shivering shocks shall break the locks of prison-gates, and Phibbus' car shall shine from far, and make and mar the foolish Fates. This was lofty. Now name the rest of the players. This is Ercles' vein, a tyrant's vein: a lover is more condoling.

QUINCE: Francis Flute the bellows-mender.

FLUTE: Here Peter Quince.

QUINCE: Flute, you must take Thisby on you.

FLUTE: What is Thisby, a wandering knight?

QUINCE: It is the lady that Pyramus must love.

FLUTE: Nay faith, let not me play a woman, I have a beard coming.

QUINCE: That's all one, you shall play it in a mask, and you may speak as small as you will.

BOTTOM: And I may hide my face, let me play Thisby too: I'll speak in a monstrous little voice; Thisne, Thisne, Ah Pyramus my lover dear, thy Thisby dear, and Lady dear.

QUINCE: No no, you must play Pyramus, and Flute, you Thisby.

BOTTOM: Well, proceed.

QUINCE: Robin Starveling the tailor.

STARVELING: Here Peter Quince.

QUINCE: Robin Starveling, you must play Thisby's mother. Tom Snout, the tinker.

SNOUT: Here Peter Quince.

QUINCE: You, Pyramus' father; myself, Thisby's father; Snug the joiner, you the Lion's part: and I hope here is a play fitted.

SNUG: Have you the Lion's part written? pray you if it be, give it me, for I am slow of study.

QUINCE: You may do it extempore, for it is nothing but roaring.

BOTTOM: Let me play the Lion too, I will roar that I will do any man's heart good to hear me. I will roar, that I will make the Duke say, Let him roar again, let him roar again.

QUINCE: And you should do it too terribly, you would fright the Duchess and the Ladies, that they would shriek, and that were enough to hang us all.

ALL: That would hang us every mother's son.

BOTTOM: I grant you friends, if you should fright the Ladies out of their wits, they would have no more discretion but to hang us: but I will aggravate my voice so, that I will roar you as gently as any sucking dove; I will roar you and 'twere any nightingale.

QUINCE: You can play no part but Pyramus, for Pyramus is a sweet-fac'd man, a proper man as one shall see in a summer's day; a most lovely gentleman-like man, therefore you must needs play Pyramus.

BOTTOM: Well, I will undertake it. What beard were I best to play it in?

QUINCE: Why, what you will.

BOTTOM: I will discharge it, in either your straw colour beard, your orange tawny beard, your purple in grain beard, or your French-crown colour'd beard, your perfect yellow.

QUINCE: Some of your French crowns have no hair at all, and then you will play bare-fac'd. But masters here are

your parts, and I am to entreat you, request you, and
desire you, to con them by tomorrow night: and meet
me in the palace wood, a mile without the town, by
moonlight; there will we rehearse: for if we meet in the
city, we shall be dogg'd with company, and our devices
known. In the mean time, I will draw a bill of properties,
such as our play wants. I pray you fail me not.

BOTTOM: We will meet, and there we may rehearse most
obscenely and courageously. Take pains, be perfect,
adieu.

QUINCE: At the Duke's oak we meet.

BOTTOM: Enough, hold or cut bow-strings.

Exeunt.

II. 1

Enter a Fairy at one door, and Robin Goodfellow at another.

ROBIN: How now spirit, whither wander you?

FAIRY: Over hill, over dale,
Thorough bush, thorough brier,
Over park, over pale,
Thorough flood, thorough fire,
I do wander every where,
Swifter than the Moon's sphere;
And I serve the Fairy Queen,
To dew her orbs upon the green.
The cowslips tall, her pensioners be,
In their gold coats, spots you see,
Those be rubies, fairy favours,
In those freckles, live their savours,
I must go seek some dewdrops here,
And hang a pearl in every cowslip's ear.
Farewell thou Lob of spirits, I'll be gone,

Our Queen and all her elves come here anon.
ROBIN: The King doth keep his revels here tonight,
   Take heed the Queen come not within his sight,
   For Oberon is passing fell and wrath,
   Because that she, as her attendant, hath
   A lovely boy stolen from an Indian King,
   She never had so sweet a changeling,
   And jealous Oberon would have the child
   Knight of his train, to trace the forests wild.
   But she (perforce) withholds the loved boy,
   Crowns him with flowers, and makes him all her joy.
   And now they never meet in grove, or green,
   By fountain clear, or spangled starlight sheen,
   But they do square, that all their elves for fear
   Creep into acorn cups and hide them there.
FAIRY: Either I mistake your shape and making quite,
   Or else you are that shrewd and knavish sprite
   Call'd Robin Goodfellow. Are not you he,
   That frights the maidens of the villagery,
   Skim milk, and sometimes labour in the quern,
   And bootless make the breathless housewife churn,
   And sometime make the drink to bear no barm,
   Mislead night-wanderers, laughing at their harm?
   Those that Hobgoblin call you, and sweet Puck,
   You do their work, and they shall have good luck.
   Are not you he?
ROBIN: Thou speak'st aright;
   I am that merry wanderer of the night:
   I jest to Oberon, and make him smile,
   When I a fat and bean-fed horse beguile,
   Neighing in likeness of a filly foal:
   And sometime lurk I in a gossip's bowl,
   In very likeness of a roasted crab:

And when she drinks, against her lips I bob,
And on her withered dewlap pour the ale.
The wisest aunt telling the saddest tale,
Sometime for three-foot stool mistaketh me,
Then slip I from her bum, down topples she,
And tailor cries, and falls into a cough.
And then the whole quire hold their hips, and laugh,
And waxen in their mirth, and neeze, and swear,
A merrier hour was never wasted there.
But room fairy, here comes Oberon.
FAIRY: And here my mistress:
Would that he were gone.
*Enter the King of Fairies at one door with his train, and the
Queen at another with hers.*
OBERON: Ill met by moonlight,
Proud Titania.
TITANIA: What, jealous Oberon? Fairies skip hence.
I have forsworn his bed and company.
OBERON: Tarry rash wanton; am not I thy Lord?
TITANIA: Then I must be thy Lady: but I know
When thou hast stolen away from Fairy land,
And in the shape of Corin, sat all day,
Playing on pipes of corn, and versing love
To amorous Phillida. Why art thou here
Come from the farthest steppe of India?
But that forsooth the bouncing Amazon
Your buskin'd mistress, and your warrior love,
To Theseus must be wedded; and you come,
To give their bed joy and prosperity.
OBERON: How canst thou thus for shame Titania,
Glance at my credit, with Hippolyta?
Knowing I know thy love to Theseus?
Didst thou not lead him through the glimmering night

From Perigenia, whom he ravished?
And make him with fair Aegles break his faith
With Ariadne, and Antiopa?
TITANIA: These are the forgeries of jealousy:
And never since the middle summer's spring
Met we on hill, in dale, forest, or mead,
By paved fountain, or by rushy brook,
Or in the beached margent of the sea,
To dance our ringlets to the whistling wind,
But with thy brawls thou hast disturb'd our sport.
Therefore the winds, piping to us in vain,
As in revenge, have suck'd up from the sea
Contagious fogs: which falling in the land,
Have every pelting river made so proud,
That they have overborne their continents.
The ox hath therefore stretch'd his yoke in vain,
The ploughman lost his sweat, and the green corn
Hath rotted, ere his youth attain'd a beard:
The fold stands empty in the drowned field,
And crows are fatted with the murrion flock;
The nine men's morris is fill'd up with mud,
And the quaint mazes in the wanton green,
For lack of tread are undistinguishable.
The human mortals want their winter here;
No night is now with hymn or carol blest;
Therefore the Moon (the governess of floods)
Pale in her anger, washes all the air;
That rheumatic diseases do abound.
And thorough this distemperature, we see
The seasons alter; hoary-headed frosts
Fall in the fresh lap of the crimson rose,
And on old Hiems' thin and icy crown,
An odorous chaplet of sweet summer buds

Is as in mockery set. The spring, the summer,
The childing autumn, angry winter change
Their wonted liveries, and the mazed world,
By their increase, now knows not which is which;
And this same progeny of evils, comes
From our debate, from our dissension;
We are their parents and original.

OBERON: Do you amend it then, it lies in you.
Why should Titania cross her Oberon?
I do but beg a little changeling boy,
To be my henchman.

TITANIA: Set your heart at rest,
The Fairy land buys not the child of me,
His mother was a votaress of my Order,
And in the spiced Indian air, by night
Full often hath she gossip'd by my side,
And sat with me on Neptune's yellow sands,
Marking th' embarked traders on the flood,
When we have laugh'd to see the sails conceive,
And grow big-bellied with the wanton wind:
Which she with pretty and with swimming gait,
Following (her womb then rich with my young squire)
Would imitate, and sail upon the land,
To fetch me trifles, and return again,
As from a voyage, rich with merchandise.
But she being mortal, of that boy did die,
And for her sake do I rear up her boy,
And for her sake I will not part with him.

OBERON: How long within this wood intend you stay?

TITANIA: Perchance till after Theseus' wedding-day.
If you will patiently dance in our round,
And see our moonlight revels, go with us;
If not, shun me and I will spare your haunts.

OBERON: Give me that boy, and I will go with thee.

TITANIA: Not for thy Fairy Kingdom. Fairies away:
  We shall chide downright, if I longer stay.
                    Exit Titania with her train.

OBERON: Well, go thy way: thou shalt not from this
    grove,
  Till I torment thee for this injury.
  My gentle Puck come hither; thou rememb'rest
  Since once I sat upon a promontory,
  And heard a mermaid on a dolphin's back,
  Uttering such dulcet and harmonious breath,
  That the rude sea grew civil at her song,
  And certain stars shot madly from their spheres,
  To hear the sea-maid's music.

PUCK: I remember.

OBERON: That very time I saw (but thou couldst not)
  Flying between the cold Moon and the Earth,
  Cupid all arm'd; a certain aim he took
  At a fair Vestal, throned by the west,
  And loos'd his love-shaft smartly from his bow,
  As it should pierce a hundred thousand hearts:
  But I might see young Cupid's fiery shaft
  Quench'd in the chaste beams of the watery Moon;
  And the imperial Votaress passed on,
  In maiden meditation, fancy-free.
  Yet mark'd I where the bolt of Cupid fell
  It fell upon a little western flower;
  Before, milk-white; now purple with love's wound,
  And maidens call it, love-in-idleness.
  Fetch me that flower; the herb I shew'd thee once,
  The juice of it, on sleeping eye-lids laid,
  Will make or man or woman madly dote
  Upon the next live creature that it sees.

Fetch me this herb, and be thou here again,
Ere the leviathan can swim a league.

PUCK: I'll put a girdle round about the earth,
In forty minutes.

Exit.

OBERON: Having once this juice,
I'll watch Titania, when she is asleep,
And drop the liquor of it in her eyes:
The next thing then she waking looks upon,
(Be it on lion, bear, or wolf, or bull,
On meddling monkey, or on busy ape)
She shall pursue it, with the soul of love.
And ere I take this charm from off her sight
(As I can take it with another herb)
I'll make her render up her page to me.
But who comes here? I am invisible,
And I will overhear their conference.

Enter Demetrius, Helena following him.

DEMETRIUS: I love thee not, therefore pursue me not,
Where is Lysander, and fair Hermia?
The one I'll slay, the other slayeth me.
Thou told'st me they were stolen unto this wood;
And here am I, and wode within this wood,
Because I cannot meet my Hermia.
Hence, get thee gone, and follow me no more.

HELENA: You draw me, you hard-hearted adamant,
But yet you draw not iron, for my heart
Is true as steel. Leave you your power to draw,
And I shall have no power to follow you.

DEMETRIUS: Do I entice you? do I speak you fair?
Or rather do I not in plainest truth,
Tell you I do not, nor I cannot love you?

HELENA: And even for that do I love you the more;

I am your spaniel, and Demetrius,
The more you beat me, I will fawn on you.
Use me but as your spaniel; spurn me, strike me,
Neglect me, lose me; only give me leave
(Unworthy as I am) to follow you.
What worser place can I beg in your love
(And yet a place of high respect with me)
Than to be used as you use your dog.

DEMETRIUS: Tempt not too much the hatred of my spirit
For I am sick when I do look on thee.

HELENA: And I am sick when I look not on you.

DEMETRIUS: You do impeach your modesty too much,
To leave the city, and commit yourself
Into the hands of one that loves you not,
To trust the opportunity of night,
And the ill counsel of a desert place,
With the rich worth of your virginity.

HELENA: Your virtue is my privilege: for that
It is not night when I do see your face.
Therefore I think I am not in the night,
Nor doth this wood lack worlds of company,
For you in my respect are all the world.
Then how can it be said I am alone,
When all the world is here to look on me?

DEMETRIUS: I'll run from thee, and hide me in the brakes,
And leave thee to the mercy of wild beasts.

HELENA: The wildest hath not such a heart as you;
Run when you will, the story shall be chang'd:
Apollo flies, and Daphne holds the chase;
The dove pursues the griffin, the mild hind
Makes speed to catch the tiger. Bootless speed,
When cowardice pursues, and valour flies.

DEMETRIUS: I will not stay thy questions, let me go;

Or if thou follow me, do not believe,
But I shall do thee mischief in the wood.

HELENA: Ay, in the temple, in the town, the field
You do me mischief. Fie Demetrius,
Your wrongs do set a scandal on my sex:
We cannot fight for love, as men may do;
We should be woo'd, and were not made to woo.

Exit Demetrius.

I'll follow thee, and make a heaven of hell,
To die upon the hand I love so well.

Exit.

OBERON: Fare thee well nymph, ere he do leave this grove,
Thou shalt fly him, and he shall seek thy love.
Hast thou the flower there? Welcome wanderer.

Enter Puck.

PUCK: Ay, there it is.

OBERON: I pray thee give it me.
I know a bank where the wild thyme blows,
Where oxlips and the nodding violet grows,
Quite over-canopied with luscious woodbine,
With sweet musk-roses, and with eglantine;
There sleeps Titania, sometime of the night,
Lull'd in these flowers, with dances and delight:
And there the snake throws her enamell'd skin,
Weed wide enough to wrap a fairy in.
And with the juice of this I'll streak her eyes,
And make her full of fateful fantasies.
Take thou some of it, and seek through this grove;
A sweet Athenian lady is in love
With a disdainful youth: anoint his eyes,
But do it when the next thing he espies,
May be the Lady. Thou shalt know the man,
By the Athenian garments he hath on.

Effect it with some care, that he may prove
More fond on her, than she upon her love;
And look thou meet me ere the first cock crow.
PUCK: Fear not my Lord, your servant shall do so.
Exeunt.

II.2

Enter Titania, Queen of Fairies, with her train.
TITANIA: Come, now a roundel, and a fairy song;
Then for the third part of a minute hence,
Some to kill cankers in the musk-rose buds,
Some war with reremice, for their leathern wings,
To make my small elves coats, and some keep back
The clamorous owl that nightly hoots and wonders
At our quaint spirits: sing me now asleep,
Then to your offices, and let me rest.
Fairies Sing.
You spotted snakes with double tongue,
Thorny hedgehogs be not seen,
Newts and blind-worms do no wrong,
Come not near our Fairy Queen.
Philomel with melody,
Sing in our sweet lullaby,
Lulla, lulla, lullaby, lulla, lulla, lullaby,
Never harm, nor spell, nor charm,
Come our lovely Lady nigh.
So good night with lullaby.
SECOND FAIRY: *Weaving spiders come not here,*
Hence you long-legg'd spinners, hence:
Beetles black approach not near;
Worm nor snail do no offence.
Philomel with melody, &c.

FIRST FAIRY: *Hence away, now all is well;*
  One aloof, stand sentinel.

  Exeunt Fairies. Titania sleeps.
  Enter Oberon.

OBERON: What thou seest when thou dost wake,
  Do it for thy true Love take:
  Love and languish for his sake.
  Be it ounce, or cat, or bear,
  Pard, or boar with bristled hair,
  In thy eye that shall appear,
  When thou wak'st, it is thy dear.
  Wake when some vile thing is near.

  Exit.
  Enter Lysander and Hermia.

LYSANDER: Fair love, you faint with wandering in the
    wood,
  And to speak troth I have forgot our way:
  We'll rest us Hermia, if you think it good,
  And tarry for the comfort of the day.

HERMIA: Be it so Lysander; find you out a bed,
  For I upon this bank will rest my head.

LYSANDER: One turf shall serve as pillow for us both,
  One heart, one bed, two bosoms, and one troth.

HERMIA: Nay good Lysander, for my sake my dear
  Lie further off yet, do not lie so near.

LYSANDER: O take the sense sweet, of my innocence,
  Love takes the meaning, in love's conference,
  I mean that my heart unto yours is knit,
  So that but one heart we can make of it.
  Two bosoms interchained with an oath,
  So then two bosoms, and a single troth.
  Then by your side, no bed-room me deny,
  For lying so, Hermia, I do not lie.

HERMIA: Lysander riddles very prettily;
    Now much beshrew my manners and my pride,
    If Hermia meant to say, Lysander lied.
    But gentle friend, for love and courtesy
    Lie further off, in human modesty;
    Such separation, as may well be said,
    Becomes a virtuous bachelor, and a maid,
    So far be distant, and good night sweet friend;
    Thy love ne'er alter, till thy sweet life end.
LYSANDER: Amen, amen, to that fair prayer, say I,
    And then end life, when I end loyalty:
    Here is my bed, sleep give thee all his rest.
HERMIA: With half that wish, the wisher's eyes be press'd.
                  Enter Puck. They sleep.
PUCK: Through the forest have I gone,
    But Athenian found I none,
    On whose eyes I might approve
    This flower's force in stirring love.
    Night and silence: who is here?
    Weeds of Athens he doth wear:
    This is he (my master said)
    Despised the Athenian maid:
    And here the maiden sleeping sound,
    On the dank and dirty ground.
    Pretty soul, she durst not lie
    Near this lack-love, this kill-courtesy.
    Churl, upon thy eyes I throw
    All the power this charm doth owe:
    When thou wakest, let love forbid
    Sleep his seat on thy eyelid.
    So awake when I am gone:
    For I must now to Oberon.
                     Exit.

Enter Demetrius and Helena running.

HELENA: Stay, though thou kill me, sweet Demetrius.

DEMETRIUS: I charge thee hence, and do not haunt me
thus.

HELENA: O wilt thou darkling leave me? do not so.

DEMETRIUS: Stay on thy peril, I alone will go.

Exit Demetrius.

HELENA: O I am out of breath, in this fond chase,
The more my prayer, the lesser is my grace.
Happy is Hermia, wheresoe'er she lies;
For she hath blessed and attractive eyes.
How came her eyes so bright? Not with salt tears:
If so, my eyes are oftener wash'd than hers.
No, no, I am as ugly as a bear;
For beasts that meet me, run away for fear.
Therefore no marvel, though Demetrius
Do as a monster, fly my presence thus.
What wicked and dissembling glass of mine,
Made me compare with Hermia's sphery eyne?
But who is here? Lysander on the ground;
Dead or asleep? I see no blood, no wound,
Lysander, if you live, good sir awake.

LYSANDER: And run through fire I will for thy sweet sake.
Transparent Helena, Nature shews her art,
That through thy bosom makes me see thy heart.
Where is Demetrius? Oh how fit a word
Is that vile name, to perish on my sword!

HELENA: Do not say so Lysander, say not so:
What though he love your Hermia? Lord, what though?
Yet Hermia still loves you; then be content.

LYSANDER: Content with Hermia? No, I do repent
The tedious minutes I with her have spent.
Not Hermia, but Helena I love;

Who will not change a raven for a dove?
The will of man is by his reason sway'd:
And reason says you are the worthier maid.
Things growing are not ripe until their season;
So I being young, till now ripe not to reason,
And touching now the point of human skill,
Reason becomes the marshal to my will,
And leads me to your eyes, where I o'erlook
Love's stories, written in Love's richest book.

HELENA: Wherefore was I to this keen mockery born?
When at your hands did I deserve this scorn?
Is't not enough, is't not enough, young man,
That I did never, no nor never can,
Deserve a sweet look from Demetrius' eye,
But you must flout my insufficiency?
Good troth you do me wrong (good sooth **you do**)
In such disdainful manner, me to woo.
But fare you well; perforce I must confess,
I thought you Lord of more true gentleness.
Oh, that a Lady of one man refus'd,
Should of another therefore be abus'd.

Exit.

LYSANDER: She sees not Hermia: Hermia sleep thou there,
And never mayst thou come Lysander near;
For as a surfeit of the sweetest things
The deep'st loathing to the stomach brings:
Or as the heresies that men do leave,
Are hated most of those they did deceive:
So thou, my surfeit, and my heresy,
Of all be hated; but the most of me;
And all my powers address your love **and might**,
To honour Helen, and to be her knight.

Exit.

HERMIA: Help me Lysander, help me; do thy best
To pluck this crawling serpent from my breast.
Ay me, for pity; what a dream was here?
Lysander look, how I do quake with fear:
Methought a serpent eat my heart away,
And you sat smiling at his cruel prey.
Lysander, what remov'd? Lysander, Lord,
What, out of hearing, gone? No sound, no word?
Alack where are you? Speak and if you hear:
Speak of all loves; I swoon almost with fear.
No, then I will perceive you are not nigh,
Either death or you I'll find immediately.

Exit.

III. 1

Enter the Clowns.

BOTTOM: Are we all met?

QUINCE: Pat, pat, and here's a marvellous convenient place for our rehearsal. This green plot shall be our stage, this hawthorn-brake our tiring-house, and we will do it in action, as we will do it before the Duke.

BOTTOM: Peter Quince?

QUINCE: What sayest thou, Bully Bottom?

BOTTOM: There are things in this Comedy of Pyramus and Thisby, that will never please. First, Pyramus must draw a sword to kill himself; which the Ladies cannot abide. How answer you that?

SNOUT: By 'r lakin, a parlous fear.

STARVELING: I believe we must leave the killing out, when all is done.

BOTTOM: Not a whit, I have a device to make all well.

Write me a Prologue, and let the Prologue seem to say, we will do no harm with our swords, and that Pyramus is not kill'd indeed: and for the more better assurance, tell them, that I Pyramus am not Pyramus, but Bottom the weaver; this will put them out of fear.

QUINCE: Well, we will have such a Prologue, and it shall be written in eight and six.

BOTTOM: No, make it two more, let it be written in eight and eight.

SNOUT: Will not the Ladies be afear'd of the Lion?

STARVELING: I fear it, I promise you.

BOTTOM: Masters, you ought to consider with yourselves, to bring in (God shield us) a Lion among Ladies is a most dreadful thing. For there is not a more fearful wild fowl than your Lion living: and we ought to look to't.

SNOUT: Therefore another Prologue must tell he is not a Lion.

BOTTOM: Nay, you must name his name, and half his face must be seen through the Lion's neck, and he himself must speak through, saying thus, or to the same defect; Ladies, or Fair Ladies, I would wish you, or I would request you, or I would entreat you, not to fear, not to tremble: my life for yours. If you think I come hither as a Lion, it were pity of my life. No, I am no such thing, I am a man as other men are; and there indeed let him name his name, and tell them plainly he is Snug the joiner.

QUINCE: Well, it shall be so; but there is two hard things, that is, to bring the moonlight into a chamber: for you know, Pyramus and Thisby meet by moonlight.

SNOUT: Doth the Moon shine that night we play our play?

BOTTOM: A Calendar, a calendar, look in the Almanac, find out moonshine, find out moonshine.

QUINCE: Yes, it doth shine that night.

BOTTOM: Why then may you leave a casement of the great chamber window (where we play) open, and the Moon may shine in at the casement.

QUINCE: Ay, or else one must come in with a bush of thorns and a lanthorn, and say he comes to disfigure, or to present the person of Moonshine. Then there is another thing, we must have a wall in the great chamber; for Pyramus and Thisby (says the story) did talk through the chink of a wall.

SNOUT: You can never bring in a wall. What say you Bottom?

BOTTOM: Some man or other must present wall, and let him have some plaster, or some loam, or some rough-cast about him, to signify wall; or let him hold his fingers thus; and through that cranny, shall Pyramus and Thisby whisper.

QUINCE: If that may be, then all is well. Come, sit down every mother's son, and rehearse your parts. Pyramus, you begin; when you have spoken your speech, enter into that brake, and so every one according to his cue.

Enter Puck.

PUCK: What hempen home-spuns have we swaggering here,
So near the cradle of the Fairy Queen?
What, a play toward? I'll be an auditor,
An actor too perhaps, if I see cause.

QUINCE: Speak Pyramus: Thisby stand forth.

PYRAMUS: Thisby, the flowers of odious savours sweet

QUINCE: Odours, odorous.

PYRAMUS: Odours savours sweet,

So hath thy breath, my dearest Thisby dear.
But hark, a voice: stay thou but here a while,
And by and by I will to thee appear.
Exit Pyramus.

PUCK: A stranger Pyramus, than e'er play'd here.
Exit.

THISBY: Must I speak now?

QUINCE: Ay marry must you. For you must understand
he goes but to see a noise that he heard and is to come
again.

THISBY: Most radiant Pyramus, most lily-white of hue,
Of colour like the red rose on triumphant brier,
Most brisky juvenal, and eke most lovely Jew,
As true as truest horse, that yet would never tire,
I'll meet thee Pyramus, at Ninny's tomb.

QUINCE: Ninus' tomb man: why, you must not speak that
yet; that you answer to Pyramus: you speak all your
part at once, cues and all. Pyramus enter, your cue is past;
it is never tire.

THISBY: O, As true as truest horse, that yet would never tire.
Enter Puck and Pyramus with the ass head.

PYRAMUS: If I were fair, Thisby, I were only thine.

QUINCE: O monstrous. O strange. We are haunted;
pray masters, fly, masters, help.
The Clowns all exit.

PUCK: I'll follow you, I'll lead you about a round,
Through bog, through bush, through brake, through
brier,
Sometime a horse I'll be, sometime a hound:
A hog, a headless bear, sometime a fire,
And neigh, and bark, and grunt, and roar, and burn,
Like horse, hound, hog, bear, fire, at every turn.
Exit.

BOTTOM: Why do they run away? this is a knavery of them to make me afeard.

Enter Snout.

SNOUT: O Bottom, thou art chang'd; what do I see on thee?

BOTTOM: What do you see? You see an ass-head of your own, do you?

Exit Snout.

Enter Quince.

QUINCE: Bless thee Bottom, bless thee; thou art translated.

Exit.

BOTTOM: I see their knavery; this is to make an ass of me, to fright me, if they could; but I will not stir from this place, do what they can. I will walk up and down here, and I will sing that they shall hear I am not afraid.

> The woosell cock, so black of hue,
> With orange-tawny bill,
> The throstle, with his note so true,
> The wren, with little quill.

TITANIA: What angel wakes me from my flowery bed?

BOTTOM: The finch, the sparrow, and the lark,
> The plain-song cuckoo grey;
> Whose note full many a man doth mark,
> And dares not answer, nay.

For indeed, who would set his wit to so foolish a bird? Who would give a bird the lie, though he cry cuckoo, never so?

TITANIA: I pray thee gentle mortal, sing again,
Mine ear is much enamour'd of thy note;
So is mine eye enthralled to thy shape,
And thy fair virtue's force (perforce) doth move me,
On the first view to say, to swear I love thee.

BOTTOM: Methinks mistress, you should have little reason
for that: and yet to say the truth, reason and love keep
little company together, now-a-days. The more the pity,
that some honest neighbours will not make them friends.
Nay, I can gleek upon occasion.

TITANIA: Thou art as wise, as thou art beautiful.

BOTTOM: Not so neither: but if I had wit enough to get
out of this wood, I have enough to serve mine own turn.

TITANIA: Out of this wood, do not desire to go,
Thou shalt remain here, whether thou wilt or no.
I am a spirit of no common rate:
The summer still doth tend upon my state,
And I do love thee; therefore go with me,
I'll give thee Fairies to attend on thee;
And they shall fetch thee jewels from the deep,
And sing, while thou on pressed flowers dost sleep:
And I will purge thy mortal grossness so,
That thou shalt like an airy spirit go.
Peaseblossom, Cobweb, Moth, and Mustardseed!
Enter Four Fairies.

FIRST FAIRY: Ready.

SECOND FAIRY: And I.

THIRD FAIRY: And I.

FOURTH FAIRY: And I.

ALL: Where shall we go?

TITANIA: Be kind and courteous to this gentleman,
Hop in his walks, and gambol in his eyes,
Feed him with apricocks, and dewberries,
With purple grapes, green figs, and mulberries,
The honey-bags steal from the humble bees,
And for night-tapers crop their waxen thighs,
And light them at the fiery glow-worm's eyes,
To have my love to bed, and to arise:

And pluck the wings from painted butterflies,
To fan the moonbeams from his sleeping eyes,
Nod to him elves, and do him courtesies.

FIRST FAIRY: Hail mortal, hail.

SECOND FAIRY: Hail.

THIRD FAIRY: Hail.

BOTTOM: I cry your worships mercy heartily; I beseech
your worship's name.

COBWEB: Cobweb.

BOTTOM: I shall desire you of more acquaintance, good
Master Cobweb: if I cut my finger, I shall make bold
with you. Your name honest gentleman?

PEASEBLOSSOM: Peaseblossom.

BOTTOM: I pray you commend me to Mistress Squash,
your mother, and to Master Peascod your father. Good
Master Peaseblossom, I shall desire of you more acquaintance too. Your name I beseech you sir?

MUSTARDSEED: Mustardseed.

BOTTOM: Good Master Mustardseed, I know your
patience well: that same cowardly giant-like ox-beef
hath devoured many a gentleman of your house. I
promise you, your kindred hath made my eyes water ere
now. I desire you more acquaintance, good Master
Mustardseed.

TITANIA: Come wait upon him, lead him to my bower.
The Moon methinks, looks with a watery eye,
And when she weeps, weeps every little flower,
Lamenting some enforced chastity.
Tie up my love's tongue, bring him silently.

Exeunt.

III. 2

Entér Oberon, solus.

OBERON: I wonder if Titania be awak'd;
  Then what it was that next came in her eye,
  Which she must dote on, in extremity.

Enter Puck.

  Here comes my messenger: how now mad spirit,
  What night-rule now about this haunted grove?
PUCK: My Mistress with a monster is in love,
  Near to her close and consecrated bower,
  While she was in her dull and sleeping hour,
  A crew of patches, rude mechanicals,
  That work for bread upon Athenian stalls,
  Were met together to rehearse a play,
  Intended for great Theseus' nuptial-day:
  The shallowest thick-skin of that barren sort,
  Who Pyramus presented, in their sport,
  Forsook his scene, and enter'd in a brake,
  When I did him at this advantage take,
  An ass's nole I fixed on his head.
  Anon his Thisbe must be answered,
  And forth my mimic comes: when they him spy,
  As wild geese, that the creeping fowler eye,
  Or russet-pated choughs, many in sort
  (Rising and cawing at the gun's report)
  Sever themselves, and madly sweep the sky:
  So at his sight, away his fellows fly,
  And at our stamp, here o'er and o'er one falls;
  He murther cries, and help from Athens calls.
  Their sense thus weak, lost with their fears thus strong,
  Made senseless things begin to do them wrong.

For briers and thorns at their apparel snatch,
Some sleeves, some hats, from yielders all things catch.
I led them on in this distracted fear,
And left sweet Pyramus translated there:
When in that moment (so it came to pass)
Titania waked, and straightway loved an ass.

OBERON: This falls out better than I could devise:
But hast thou yet latch'd the Athenian's eyes,
With a love-juice, as I did bid thee do?

PUCK: I took him sleeping (that is finish'd too)
And the Athenian woman by his side,
That when he wak'd, of force she must be eyed.

Enter Hermia and Demetrius.

OBERON: Stand close, this is the same Athenian.

PUCK: This is the woman, but not this the man.

DEMETRIUS: O why rebuke you him that loves you so?
Lay breath so bitter on your bitter foe.

HERMIA: Now I but chide, but I should use thee worse.
For thou (I fear) hast given me cause to curse,
If thou hast slain Lysander in his sleep,
Being o'er shoes in blood, plunge in the deep,
And kill me too:
The sun was not so true unto the day.
As he to me. Would he have stolen away,
From sleeping Hermia? I'll believe as soon
This whole earth may be bor'd, and that the Moon
May through the centre creep, and so displease
Her brother's noontide, with th' Antipodes.
It cannot be but thou hast murder'd him,
So should a murtherer look, so dead, so grim.

DEMETRIUS: So should the murder'd look; and so
should I,
Pierced through the heart with your stern cruelty:

Yet you the murtherer look as bright as clear,
As yonder Venus in her glimmering sphere.

HERMIA: What's this to my Lysander? where is he?
Ah good Demetrius, wilt thou give him me?

DEMETRIUS: I had rather give his carcass to my hounds.

HERMIA: Out dog, out cur, thou drivest me past the
bounds
Of maiden's patience. Hast thou slain him then?
Henceforth be never number'd among men.
Oh, once tell true, tell true, even for my sake,
Durst thou have look'd upon him, being awake?
And hast thou kill'd him sleeping? O brave touch:
Could not a worm, an adder do so much?
An adder did it: for with doubler tongue
Than thine (thou serpent) never adder stung.

DEMETRIUS: You spend your passion on a mispris'd mood,
I am not guilty of Lysander's blood:
Nor is he dead for aught that I can tell.

HERMIA: I pray thee tell me then that he is well.

DEMETRIUS: And if I could, what should I get therefore?

HERMIA: A privilege, never to see me more;
And from thy hated presence part I so:
See me no more whether he be dead or no.
                              Exit.

DEMETRIUS: There is no following her in this fierce vein,
Here therefore for a while I will remain.
So sorrow's heaviness doth heavier grow:
For debt that bankrupt sleep doth sorrow owe,
Which now in some slight measure it will pay,
If for his tender here I make some stay.
                         Lies down.

OBERON: What hast thou done? Thou hast mistaken quite
And laid the love-juice on some true-love's sight:

Of thy misprision, must perforce ensue
Some true love turn'd, and not a false turn'd true.
PUCK: Then fate o'er-rules, that one man holding troth,
A million fail, confounding oath on oath.
OBERON: About the wood, go swifter than the wind,
And Helena of Athens look thou find.
All fancy-sick she is, and pale of cheer,
With sighs of love, that costs the fresh blood dear.
By some illusion see thou bring her here,
I'll charm his eyes against she do appear.
PUCK: I go, I go, look how I go,
Swifter than arrow from the Tartar's bow.

Exit.

OBERON: Flower of this purple dye,
Hit with Cupid's archery,
Sink in apple of his eye,
When his love he doth espy,
Let her shine as gloriously
As the Venus of the sky.
When thou wak'st if she be by,
Beg of her for remedy.

Enter Puck.

PUCK: Captain of our Fairy band,
Helena is here at hand,
And the youth, mistook by me,
Pleading for a lover's fee.
Shall we their fond pageant see?
Lord, what fools these mortals be!
OBERON: Stand aside: the noise they make,
Will cause Demetrius to awake.
PUCK: Then will two at once woo one,
That must needs be sport alone:
And those things do best please me,

That befal preposterously.
Exeunt.
Enter Lysander and Helena.

LYSANDER: Why should you think that I should woo in
 scorn?
 Scorn and derision never comes in tears:
 Look when I vow I weep; and vows so born,
 In their nativity all truth appears.
 How can these things in me, seem scorn to you?
 Bearing the badge of faith to prove them true.

HELENA: You do advance your cunning more and more,
 When truth kills truth, O devilish-holy fray!
 These vows are Hermia's. Will you give her o'er?
 Weigh oath with oath, and you will nothing weigh.
 Your vows to her, and me, (put in two scales)
 Will even weigh, and both as light as tales.

LYSANDER: I had no judgement, when to her I swore.

HELENA: Nor none in my mind, now you give her o'er.

LYSANDER: Demetrius loves her, and he loves not you.
Demetrius awakes.

DEMETRIUS: O Helen, goddess, nymph, perfect, divine,
 To what my love, shall I compare thine eyne?
 Crystal is muddy, O how ripe in show,
 Thy lips, those kissing cherries, tempting grow!
 That pure congealed white, high Taurus' snow,
 Fann'd with the eastern wind, turns to a crow,
 When thou hold'st up thy hand. O let me kiss
 This Princess of pure white, this seal of bliss.

HELENA: O spite! O hell! I see you all are bent
 To set against me, for your merriment:
 If you were civil, and knew courtesy,
 You would not do me thus much injury.
 Can you not hate me, as I know you do,

But you must join in souls to mock me too?
If you were men, as men you are in show,
You would not use a gentle Lady so;
To vow, and swear, and superpraise my parts,
When I am sure you hate me with your hearts.
You both are rivals, and love Hermia;
And now both rivals to mock Helena.
A trim exploit, a manly enterprise,
To conjure tears up in a poor maid's eyes,
With your derision; none of noble sort,
Would so offend a virgin, and extort
A poor soul's patience, all to make you sport.

LYSANDER: You are unkind, Demetrius; be not so,
For you love Hermia; this you know I know;
And here with all good will, with all my heart,
In Hermia's love I yield you up my part;
And yours of Helena, to me bequeath,
Whom I do love, and will do till my death.

HELENA: Never did mockers waste more idle breath.

DEMETRIUS: Lysander, keep thy Hermia, I will none:
If e'er I lov'd her, all that love is gone.
My heart to her, but as guest-wise sojourn'd,
And now to Helen is it home return'd,
There to remain.

LYSANDER: Helen, it is not so.

DEMETRIUS: Disparage not the faith thou dost not know,
Lest to thy peril thou aby it dear.
Look where thy love comes, yonder is thy dear.
                    Enter Hermia.

HERMIA: Dark night, that from the eye his function takes,
The ear more quick of apprehension makes,
Wherein it doth impair the seeing sense,
It pays the hearing double recompense.

Thou art not by mine eye, Lysander found,
Mine ear (I thank it) brought me to thy sound.
But why unkindly didst thou leave me so?
LYSANDER: Why should he stay whom Love doth press
to go?
HERMIA: What love could press Lysander from my side?
LYSANDER: Lysander's love (that would not let him bide)
Fair Helena; who more engilds the night,
Than all yon fiery oes, and eyes of light.
Why seek'st thou me? could not this make thee know,
The hate I bare thee, made me leave thee so?
HERMIA: You speak not as you think; it cannot be.
HELENA: Lo, she is one of this confederacy.
Now I perceive they have conjoin'd all three,
To fashion this false sport in spite of me.
Injurious Hermia, most ungrateful maid,
Have you conspir'd, have you with these contriv'd
To bait me, with this foul derision?
Is all the counsel that we two have shar'd,
The sisters' vows, the hours that we have spent,
When we have chid the hasty-footed time,
For parting us; O, is all forgot?
All school-days' friendship, childhood innocence?
We Hermia, like two artificial gods,
Have with our needles, created both one flower,
Both on one sampler, sitting on one cushion,
Both warbling of one song, both in one key;
As if our hands, our sides, voices, and minds
Had been incorporate. So we grew together
Like to a double cherry, seeming parted,
But yet an union in partition,
Two lovely berries, moulded on one stem,
So with two seeming bodies, but one heart,

Two of the first like coats in heraldry,
Due but to one and crowned with one crest.
And will you rent our ancient love asunder,
To join with men in scorning your poor friend?
It is not friendly, 'tis not maidenly.
Our sex as well as I, may chide you for it,
Though I alone do feel the injury.

HERMIA: I am amazed at your passionate words,
I scorn you not; it seems that you scorn me.

HELENA: Have you not set Lysander, as in scorn
To follow me, and praise my eyes and face?
And made your other love, Demetrius
(Who even but now did spurn me with his foot)
To call me goddess, nymph, divine, and rare,
Precious, celestial? Wherefore speaks he this
To her he hates? And wherefore doth Lysander
Deny your love (so rich within his soul)
And tender me (forsooth) affection,
But by your setting on, by your consent?
What though I be not so in grace as you,
So hung upon with love, so fortunate?
(But miserable most, to love unlov'd)
This you should pity, rather than despise.

HERMIA: I understand not what you mean by this.

HELENA: Ay, do, persever, counterfeit sad looks,
Make mouths upon me when I turn my back,
Wink each at other, hold the sweet jest up:
This sport well carried, shall be chronicled.
If you have any pity, grace, or manners,
You would not make me such an argument:
But fare ye well, 'tis partly my own fault,
Which death or absence soon shall remedy.

LYSANDER: Stay gentle Helena, hear my excuse,

My love, my life, my soul, fair Helena.

HELENA: O excellent!

HERMIA: Sweet, do not scorn her so.

DEMETRIUS: If she cannot entreat, I can compel.

LYSANDER: Thou canst compel, no more than she entreat.

Thy threats have no more strength than her weak prayers.

Helen, I love thee, by my life I do;

I swear by that which I will lose for thee,

To prove him false, that says I love thee not.

DEMETRIUS: I say, I love thee more than he can do.

LYSANDER: If thou say so, withdraw and prove it too.

DEMETRIUS: Quick, come.

HERMIA: Lysander, whereto tends all this?

LYSANDER: Away, you Ethiope.

DEMETRIUS: No, no, sir, seem to break loose:

Take on as you would follow,

But yet come not: you are a tame man, go.

LYSANDER: Hang off thou cat, thou burr; vile thing let loose,

Or I will shake thee from me like a serpent.

HERMIA: Why are you grown so rude?

What change is this sweet love?

LYSANDER: Thy love? out tawny Tartar, out;

Out loathed medicine; hated potion, hence.

HERMIA: Do you not jest?

HELENA: Yes sooth, and so do you.

LYSANDER: Demetrius: I will keep my word with thee.

DEMETRIUS: I would I had your bond; for I perceive

A weak bond holds you; I'll not trust your word.

LYSANDER: What, should I hurt her, strike her, kill her dead?

Although I hate her, I'll not harm her so.

HERMIA: What, can you do me greater harm than hate?
Hate me, wherefore? O me, what news my Love?
Am not I Hermia? Are not you Lysander?
I am as fair now, as I was erewhile.
Since night you lov'd me; yet since night you left me.
Why then you left me (O the gods forbid)
In earnest, shall I say?

LYSANDER: Ay, by my life;
And never did desire to see thee more.
Therefore be out of hope, of question, of doubt;
Be certain, nothing truer: 'tis no jest,
That I do hate thee, and love Helena.

HERMIA: O me, you juggler, you canker-blossom,
You thief of love; what, have you come by night,
And stolen my love's heart from him?

HELENA: Fine i' faith:
Have you no modesty, no maiden shame,
No touch of bashfulness? What, will you tear
Impatient answers from my gentle tongue?
Fie, fie, you counterfeit, you puppet, you.

HERMIA: Puppet? why so? ay, that way goes the game.
Now I perceive that she hath made compare
Between our statures, she hath urg'd her height,
And with her personage, her tall personage,
Her height (forsooth) she hath prevail'd with him.
And are you grown so high in his esteem,
Because I am so dwarfish, and so low?
How low am I, thou painted maypole? Speak,
How low am I? I am not yet so low,
But that my nails can reach unto thine eyes.

HELENA: I pray you though you mock me, gentlemen,
Let her not hurt me; I was never curst:
I have no gift at all in shrewishness;

I am a right maid for my cowardice;
Let her not strike me: you perhaps may think,
Because she is something lower than myself,
That I can match her.

HERMIA: Lower? hark again.

HELENA: Good Hermia, do not be so bitter with me,
I evermore did love you Hermia,
Did ever keep your counsels, never wrong'd you,
Save that in love unto Demetrius,
I told him of your stealth unto this wood.
He follow'd you, for love I follow'd him,
But he hath chid me hence, and threatened me
To strike me, spurn me, nay to kill me too;
And now, so you will let me quiet go,
To Athens will I bear my folly back,
And follow you no further. Let me go.
You see how simple, and how fond I am.

HERMIA: Why get you gone: who is't that hinders you?

HELENA: A foolish heart, that I leave here behind.

HERMIA: What, with Lysander?

HELENA: With Demetrius.

LYSANDER: Be not afraid, she shall not harm thee Helena.

DEMETRIUS: No sir, she shall not, though you take her part.

HELENA: O when she's angry, she is keen and shrewd,
She was a vixen when she went to school,
And though she be but little, she is fierce.

HERMIA: Little again? nothing but low and little?
Why will you suffer her to flout me thus?
Let me come to her.

LYSANDER: Get you gone you dwarf,
You *minimus* of hindering knot-grass made,
You bead, you acorn.

DEMETRIUS: You are too officious,
In her behalf that scorns your services.
Let her alone, speak not of Helena,
Take not her part. For if thou dost intend
Never so little show of love to her,
Thou shalt aby it.

LYSANDER: Now she holds me not,
Now follow if thou darest, to try whose right,
Of thine or mine is most in Helena.

DEMETRIUS: Follow? nay, I'll go with thee cheek by jowl.
Exeunt Lysander and Demetrius.

HERMIA: You mistress, all this coil is 'long of you.
Nay, go not back.

HELENA: I will not trust you I,
Nor longer stay in your curst company.
Your hands than mine, are quicker for a fray,
My legs are longer though to run away.

HERMIA: I am amaz'd, and know not what to say.
Exeunt.
Enter Oberon and Puck.

OBERON: This is thy negligence, still thou mistak'st.
Or else committ'st thy knaveries wilfully.

PUCK: Believe me, King of shadows, I mistook.
Did not you tell me, I should know the man,
By the Athenian garments he had on?
And so far blameless proves my enterprise,
That I have 'nointed an Athenian's eyes,
And so far am I glad, it so did sort,
As this their jangling I esteem a sport.

OBERON: Thou see'st these lovers seek a place to fight.
Hie therefore Robin, overcast the night,
The starry welkin cover thou anon,
With drooping fog as black as Acheron,

And lead these testy rivals so astray,
As one come not within another's way.
Like to Lysander, sometime frame thy tongue,
Then stir Demetrius up with bitter wrong;
And sometime rail thou like Demetrius;
And from each other look thou lead them thus,
Till o'er their brows, death-counterfeiting, sleep
With leaden legs, and batty wings doth creep;
Then crush this herb into Lysander's eye,
Whose liquor hath this virtuous property,
To take from thence all error, with his might,
And make his eyeballs roll with wonted sight:
When they next wake, all this derision
Shall seem a dream, and fruitless vision,
And back to Athens shall the lovers wend,
With league, whose date till death shall never end.
Whiles I in this affair do thee employ,
I'll to my Queen, and beg her Indian boy;
And then I will her charmed eye release
From monster's view, and all things shall be peace.

PUCK: My Fairy Lord, this must be done with haste,
For night's swift dragons cut the clouds full fast,
And yonder shines Aurora's harbinger;
At whose approach ghosts wandering here and there,
Troop home to churchyards; damned spirits all,
That in crossways and floods have burial,
Already to their wormy beds are gone;
For fear lest day should look their shames upon,
They wilfully themselves exile from light,
And must for aye consort with black-brow'd night.

OBERON: But we are spirits of another sort:
I, with the morning's love have oft made sport,
And like a forester, the groves may tread,

Even till the eastern gate all fiery-red,
Opening on Neptune, with fair blessed beams,
Turns into yellow gold, his salt green streams.
But notwithstanding haste, make no delay:
We may effect this business, yet ere day.

Exit.

PUCK: Up and down, up and down,
I will lead them up and down:
I am fear'd in field and town.
Goblin, lead them up and down:
Here comes one.

Enter Lysander.

LYSANDER: Where art thou, proud Demetrius?
Speak thou now.

PUCK: Here villain, drawn and ready. Where art thou?

LYSANDER: I will be with thee straight.

PUCK: Follow me then to plainer ground.

Exit Lysander.
Enter Demetrius.

DEMETRIUS: Lysander, speak again;
Thou runaway, thou coward, art thou fled?
Speak, in some bush? Where dost thou hide thy head?

PUCK: Thou coward, art thou bragging to the stars,
Telling the bushes that thou look'st for wars,
And wilt not come? Come recreant, come thou child,
I'll whip thee with a rod. He is defil'd
That draws a sword on thee.

DEMETRIUS: Yea, art thou there?

PUCK: Follow my voice, we'll try no manhood here.

Exeunt.
Enter Lysander.

LYSANDER: He goes before me, and still dares me on,
When I come where he calls, then he is gone.

The villain is much lighter-heel'd than I:
I follow'd fast, but faster he did fly;
That fallen am I in dark uneven way,
And here will rest me. Come thou gentle day:

Lies down.

For if but once thou show me thy grey light,
I'll find Demetrius, and revenge this spite.

Enter Puck and Demetrius.

PUCK: Ho, ho, ho; coward, why com'st thou not?

DEMETRIUS: Abide me, if thou darest. For well I wot,
Thou runn'st before me, shifting every place,
And dar'st not stand, nor look me in the face.
Where art thou now?

PUCK: Come hither, I am here.

DEMETRIUS: Nay then thou mock'st me; thou shalt buy
this dear,
If ever I thy face by daylight see.
Now go thy way: faintness constraineth me,
To measure out my length on this cold bed:
By day's approach look to be visited.

Lies down and sleeps.

Enter Helena.

HELENA: O weary night, O long and tedious night,
Abate thy hours, shine comforts from the East,
That I may back to Athens by daylight,
From these that my poor company detest;
And sleep that sometimes shuts up sorrow's eye,
Steal me awhile from mine own company.

Sleeps.

PUCK: Yet but three? Come one more,
Two of both kinds makes up four.
Here she comes, curst and sad,
Cupid is a knavish lad,

Enter Hermia.

Thus to make poor females mad.

HERMIA: Never so weary, never so in woe,
Bedabbled with the dew, and torn with briers,
I can no further crawl, no further go;
My legs can keep no pace with my desires.
Here will I rest me till the break of day,
Heavens shield Lysander, if they mean a fray.

Sleeps.

PUCK: On the ground, sleep sound:
I'll apply to your eye,
Gentle lover, remedy.
When thou wak'st, thou tak'st
True delight, in the sight,
Of thy former Lady's eye:
And the country proverb known,
That every man should take his own,
In your waking shall be shown,
Jack shall have Jill:
Nought shall go ill:
The man shall have his mare again, and all shall be well.

Exit.

They sleep all the act.

IV. 1

*Enter Queen of Fairies, and Bottom, and Fairies, and the
King behind them.*

TITANIA: Come, sit thee down upon this flowery bed,
While I thy amiable cheeks do coy,
And stick musk-roses in thy sleek smooth head,
And kiss thy fair large ears, my gentle joy.

BOTTOM: Where's Peaseblossom?

PEASEBLOSSOM: Ready.

BOTTOM: Scratch my head, Peaseblossom. Where's Mounsieur Cobweb?

COBWEB: Ready.

BOTTOM: Mounsieur Cobweb, good Mounsieur get you your weapons in your hand, and kill me a red-hipped humble-bee, on the top of a thistle; and good Mounsieur bring me the honey-bag. Do not fret yourself too much in the action, Mounsieur; and good Mounsieur have a care the honey-bag break not, I would be loth to have you overflown with a honey-bag signior. Where's Mounsieur Mustardseed?

MUSTARDSEED: Ready.

BOTTOM: Give me your neaf, Mounsieur Mustardseed. Pray you leave your courtesy good Mounsieur.

MUSTARDSEED: What's your will?

BOTTOM: Nothing good Mounsieur, but to help Cavalery Cobweb to scratch. I must to the barber's Mounsieur, for methinks I am marvellous hairy about the face. And I am such a tender ass, if my hair do but tickle me, I must scratch.

TITANIA: What, wilt thou hear some music, my sweet love?

BOTTOM: I have a reasonable good ear in music. Let's have the tongs and the bones.

Music Tongs; rural music.

TITANIA: Or say sweet love, what thou desirest to eat.

BOTTOM: Truly a peck of provender; I could munch your good dry oats. Methinks I have a great desire to a bottle of hay: good hay, sweet hay hath no fellow.

TITANIA: I have a venturous Fairy, that shall seek The squirrel's hoard, and fetch thee new nuts.

BOTTOM: I had rather have a handful or two of dried peas.

But I pray you let none of your people stir me, I have an
exposition of sleep come upon me.

TITANIA: Sleep thou, and I will wind thee in my arms.
Fairies be gone, and be all ways away.

Exeunt Fairies.

So doth the woodbine the sweet honeysuckle
Gently entwist; the female ivy so
Enrings the barky fingers of the elm.
O how I love thee! how I dote on thee!

Enter Robin Goodfellow and Oberon.

OBERON: Welcome good Robin: see'st thou this sweet
sight?
Her dotage now I do begin to pity.
For meeting her of late behind the wood,
Seeking sweet favours for this hateful fool,
I did upbraid her, and fall out with her.
For she his hairy temples then had rounded,
With coronet of fresh and fragrant flowers.
And that same dew which sometime on the buds,
Was wont to swell like round and orient pearls;
Stood now within the pretty flowerets' eyes,
Like tears that did their own disgrace bewail.
When I had at my pleasure taunted her,
And she in mild terms begg'd my patience,
I then did ask of her, her changeling child,
Which straight she gave me, and her fairy sent
To bear him to my bower in Fairy Land.
And now I have the boy, I will undo
This hateful imperfection of her eyes.
And gentle Puck, take this transformed scalp,
From off the head of this Athenian swain;
That he awaking when the other do,
May all to Athens back again repair,

And think no more of this night's accidents,
But as the fierce vexation of a dream.
But first I will release the Fairy Queen.
> *Be as thou wast wont to be;*
> *See as thou wast wont to see.*
> *Dian's bud, o'er Cupid's flower,*
> *Hath such force and blessed power.*

Now my Titania wake you my sweet Queen.

TITANIA: My Oberon, what visions have I seen!
Methought I was enamour'd of an ass.

OBERON: There lies your love.

TITANIA: How came these things to pass?
Oh, how mine eyes do loathe his visage now!

OBERON: Silence awhile. Robin take off this head:
Titania, music call, and strike more dead
Than common sleep, of all these five the sense.

TITANIA: Music, ho music, such as charmeth sleep.
> *Music still.*

ROBIN: Now, when thou wak'st, with thine own fool's
eyes peep.

OBERON: Sound music; come my Queen, take hands with
me
And rock the ground whereon these sleepers be.
Now thou and I are new in amity,
And will tomorrow midnight, solemnly
Dance in Duke Theseus' house triumphantly,
And bless it to all fair prosperity.
There shall the pairs of faithful lovers be
Wedded, with Theseus, all in jollity.

PUCK: Fairy King attend, and mark,
I do hear the morning lark.

OBERON: Then my Queen in silence sad,
Trip we after night's shade;

Was never holla'd to, nor cheer'd with horn,
In Crete, in Sparta, nor in Thessaly;
Judge when you hear. But soft, what nymphs are these?
EGEUS: My Lord, this is my daughter here asleep,
And this Lysander, this Demetrius is,
This Helena, old Nedar's Helena,
I wonder of their being here together.
THESEUS: No doubt they rose up early, to observe
The rite of May; and hearing our intent,
Came here in grace of our solemnity.
But speak Egeus, is not this the day
That Hermia should give answer of her choice?
EGEUS: It is, my Lord.
THESEUS: Go bid the huntsmen wake them with their
horns.
    Wind horns. Shout within: they all start up.
Good morrow friends: Saint Valentine is past:
Begin these wood-birds but to couple now?
LYSANDER: Pardon my Lord.
THESEUS: I pray you all stand up.
I know you two are rival enemies.
How comes this gentle concord in the world,
That hatred is so far from jealousy,
To sleep by hate, and fear no enmity?
LYSANDER: My Lord, I shall reply amazedly,
Half sleep, half waking. But as yet, I swear,
I cannot truly say how I came here.
But as I think (for truly would I speak)
And now I do bethink me, so it is;
I came with Hermia hither. Our intent
Was to be gone from Athens, where we might,
Without the peril of the Athenian law.
EGEUS: Enough, enough, my Lord: you have enough;

I beg the Law, the Law, upon his head:
They would have stolen away, they would Demetrius,
Thereby to have defeated you and me:
You of your wife, and me of my consent;
Of my consent, that she should be your wife.

DEMETRIUS: My Lord, fair Helen told me of their stealth,
Of this their purpose hither, to this wood,
And I in fury hither follow'd them;
Fair Helena in fancy following me.
But my good Lord, I wot not by what power,
(But by some power it is) my love to Hermia
(Melted as the snow) seems to me now
As the remembrance of an idle gaud,
Which in my childhood I did dote upon:
And all the faith, the virtue of my heart,
The object and the pleasure of mine eye,
Is only Helena. To her, my Lord,
Was I betroth'd, ere I see Hermia,
But like in sickness did I loathe this food,
But as in health, come to my natural taste,
Now I do wish it, love it, long for it,
And will for evermore be true to it.

THESEUS: Fair lovers, you are fortunately met;
Of this discourse we more will hear anon.
Egeus, I will overbear your will;
For in the Temple, by and by with us,
These couples shall eternally be knit.
And for the morning now is something worn,
Our purpos'd hunting shall be set aside.
Away, with us to Athens; three and three,
We'll hold a feast in great solemnity.
Come Hippolyta.

Exit Duke and Lords.

DEMETRIUS: These things seem small and undistinguish-
able,
Like far-off mountains turned into clouds.
HERMIA: Methinks I see these things with parted eye,
When every thing seems double.
HELENA: So methinks:
And I have found Demetrius, like a jewel,
Mine own, and not mine own.
DEMETRIUS: Are you sure
That we are awake? It seems to me,
That yet we sleep, we dream. Do not you think,
The Duke was here, and bid us follow him?
HERMIA: Yea, and my father.
HELENA: And Hippolyta.
LYSANDER: And he did bid us follow to the Temple.
DEMETRIUS: Why then we are awake; let's follow him,
And by the way let us recount our dreams.

Exeunt lovers.
Bottom wakes.

BOTTOM: When my cue comes, call me, and I will answer.
My next is, Most fair Pyramus. Heigh-ho. Peter Quince?
Flute the bellows-mender? Snout the tinker? Starveling?
God's my life! Stolen hence, and left me asleep: I have
had a most rare vision. I have had a dream, past the wit of
man, to say, what dream it was. Man is but an ass, if he
go about to expound this dream. Methought I was,
there is no man can tell what. Methought I was, and
methought I had. But man is but a patch'd fool, if he will
offer to say, what methought I had. The eye of man hath
not heard, the ear of man hath not seen, man's hand is not
able to taste, his tongue to conceive, nor his heart to
report, what my dream was. I will get Peter Quince to
write a ballad of this dream, it shall be called *Bottom's*

Dream, because it hath no bottom; and I will sing it in
the latter end of a play, before the Duke. Peradventure,
to make it the more gracious, I shall sing it at her death.

Exit.

IV. 2

Enter Quince, Flute, Snout, and Starveling.

QUINCE: Have you sent to Bottom's house? Is he come
home yet?

STARVELING: He cannot be heard of. Out of doubt he is
transported.

FLUTE: If he come not, then the play is marr'd. It goes not
forward, doth it?

QUINCE: It is not possible: you have not a man in all
Athens, able to discharge Pyramus but he.

FLUTE: No, he hath simply the best wit of any handicraft
man in Athens.

QUINCE: Yea, and the best person too, and he is a very
paramour, for a sweet voice.

FLUTE: You must say, paragon. A paramour is (God bless
us) a thing of naught.

Enter Snug the joiner.

SNUG: Masters, the Duke is coming from the Temple,
and there is two or three Lords and Ladies more married.
If our sport had gone forward, we had all been made
men.

FLUTE: O sweet bully Bottom: thus hath he lost sixpence a
day, during his life; he could not have scaped sixpence a
day. And the Duke had not given him sixpence a day
for playing Pyramus, I'll be hang'd. He would have
deserved it. Sixpence a day in Pyramus, or nothing.

Enter Bottom.

BOTTOM: Where are these lads? Where are these hearts?

QUINCE: Bottom, O most courageous day! O most happy hour!

BOTTOM: Masters, I am to discourse wonders; but ask me not what. For if I tell you, I am no true Athenian. I will tell you every thing right as it fell out.

QUINCE: Let us hear, sweet Bottom.

BOTTOM: Not a word of me: all that I will tell you, is, that the Duke hath dined. Get your apparel together, good strings to your beards, new ribbons to your pumps, meet presently at the Palace, every man look o'er his part: for the short and the long is, our play is preferred. In any case let Thisby have clean linen: and let not him that plays the Lion, pare his nails, for they shall hang out for the Lion's claws. And most dear actors, eat no onions, nor garlic; for we are to utter sweet breath, and I do not doubt but to hear them say, it is a sweet Comedy. No more words: away, go away.

Exeunt.

V. I

Enter Theseus, Hippolyta, Philostrate and Lords.

HIPPOLYTA: 'Tis strange my Theseus, that these lovers speak of.

THESEUS: More strange than true. I never may believe
These antique fables, nor these fairy toys.
Lovers and madmen have such seething brains,
Such shaping fantasies, that apprehend
More than cool reason ever comprehends.
The Lunatic, the Lover, and the Poet,
Are of imagination all compact.
One sees more devils than vast hell can hold;

That is the Madman. The Lover, all as frantic,
Sees Helen's beauty in a brow of Egypt.
The Poet's eye, in a fine frenzy rolling,
Doth glance from heaven to earth, from earth to heaven.
And as imagination bodies forth
The forms of things unknown; the Poet's pen
Turns them to shapes, and gives to airy nothing,
A local habitation, and a name.
Such tricks hath strong imagination,
That if it would but apprehend some joy,
It comprehends some bringer of that joy.
Or in the night, imagining some fear,
How easy is a bush suppos'd a bear?

HIPPOLYTA: But all the story of the night told over,
And all their minds transfigur'd so together,
More witnesseth than fancy's images,
And grows to something of great constancy;
But howsoever, strange, and admirable.

Enter lovers, Lysander, Demetrius, Hermia, and Helena.

THESEUS: Here come the lovers, full of joy and mirth:
Joy, gentle friends, joy and fresh days of love
Accompany your hearts.

LYSANDER: More than to us,
Wait in your royal walks, your board, your bed.

THESEUS: Come now, what masques, what dances shall
we have,
To wear away this long age of three hours,
Between our after-supper, and bed-time?
Where is our usual manager of mirth?
What revels are in hand? Is there no play,
To ease the anguish of a torturing hour?
Call Philostrate.

PHILOSTRATE: Here mighty Theseus.

THESEUS: Say, what abridgement have you for this
    evening?
  What masque? What music? How shall we beguile
  The lazy time, if not with some delight?
PHILOSTRATE: There is a brief how many sports are ripe:
  Make choice of which your Highness will see first.
LYSANDER: The battle with the Centaurs, to be sung
  By an Athenian eunuch, to the harp.
THESEUS: We'll none of that. That have I told my Love
  In glory of my kinsman Hercules.
LYSANDER: The riot of the tipsy Bacchanals,
  Tearing the Thracian singer, in their rage.
THESEUS: That is an old device, and it was play'd
  When I from Thebes came last a conqueror.
LYSANDER: The thrice three Muses, mourning for the
    death
  Of Learning, late deceas'd in beggary.
THESEUS: That is some satire keen and critical,
  Not sorting with a nuptial ceremony.
LYSANDER: A tedious brief scene of young Pyramus,
  And his love Thisbe; very tragical mirth.
THESEUS: Merry and tragical? tedious, and brief?
  That is, hot ice, and wondrous strange snow.
  How shall we find the concord of this discord?
PHILOSTRATE: A play there is, my Lord, some ten words
    long,
  Which is as brief as I have known a play;
  But by ten words, my Lord, it is too long;
  Which makes it tedious. For in all the play,
  There is not one word apt, one player fitted.
  And tragical my noble Lord it is:
  For Pyramus therein doth kill himself.
  Which when I saw rehears'd, I must confess,

Made mine eyes water: but more merry tears,
The passion of loud laughter never shed.

THESEUS: What are they that do play it?

PHILOSTRATE: Hard-handed men, that work in Athens
here,
Which never labour'd in their minds till now;
And now have toil'd their unbreathed memories
With this same play, against your nuptial.

THESEUS: And we will hear it.

PHILOSTRATE: No, my noble Lord,
It is not for you. I have heard it over,
And it is nothing, nothing in the world;
Unless you can find sport in their intents,
Extremely stretch'd, and conn'd with cruel pain,
To do you service.

THESEUS: I will hear that play.
For never any thing can be amiss,
When simpleness and duty tender it.
Go bring them in, and take your places, Ladies.

Exit Philostrate.

HIPPOLYTA: I love not to see wretchedness o'ercharged;
And duty in his service perishing.

THESEUS: Why gentle sweet, you shall see no such thing.

HIPPOLYTA: He says, they can do nothing in this kind.

THESEUS: The kinder we, to give them thanks for nothing.
Our sport shall be, to take what they mistake;
And what poor duty cannot do, noble respect
Takes it in might, not merit.
Where I have come, great clerks have purposed
To greet me with premeditated welcomes;
Where I have seen them shiver and look pale,
Make periods in the midst of sentences,
Throttle their practis'd accent in their fears.

And in conclusion, dumbly have broke off,
Not paying me a welcome. Trust me sweet,
Out of this silence yet, I pick'd a welcome:
And in the modesty of fearful duty,
I read as much, as from the rattling tongue
Of saucy and audacious eloquence.
Love therefore, and tongue-tied simplicity,
In least, speak most, to my capacity.
Enter Philostrate.

PHILOSTRATE: So please your Grace, the Prologue is adress'd.

THESEUS: Let him approach.
Flourish of trumpets.
Enter the Prologue (Quince).

PROLOGUE: If we offend, it is with our good will.
That you should think, we come not to offend,
But with good will. To show our simple skill,
That is the true beginning of our end.
Consider then, we come but in despite.
We do not come, as minding to content you,
Our true intent is. All for your delight,
We are not here. That you should here repent you,
The actors are at hand: and by their show,
You shall know all, that you are like to know.

THESEUS: This fellow doth not stand upon points.

LYSANDER: He hath rid his Prologue, like a rough colt: he knows not the stop. A good moral my Lord. It is not enough to speak, but to speak true.

HIPPOLYTA: Indeed he hath played on his Prologue, like a child on a recorder, a sound, but not in government.

THESEUS: His speech was like a tangled chain: nothing impaired, but all disordered. Who is next?
Enter Pyramus and Thisbe, Wall, Moonshine, and Lion.

PROLOGUE: Gentles, perchance you wonder at this show,
  But wonder on, till truth make all things plain.
  This man is Pyramus, if you would know;
  This beauteous Lady, Thisby is certain.
  This man, with lime and rough-cast, doth present
  Wall, that vile Wall, which did these lovers sunder:
  And through Wall's chink (poor souls) they are content
  To whisper. At the which, let no man wonder.
  This man, with lanthorn, dog, and bush of thorn,
  Presenteth Moonshine. For if you will know,
  By moonshine did these lovers think no scorn
  To greet at Ninus' tomb, there, there to woo:
  This grisly beast (which Lion hight by name)
  The trusty Thisby, coming first by night,
  Did scare away, or rather did affright:
  And as she fled, her mantle she did fall;
  Which Lion vile with bloody mouth did stain.
  Anon comes Pyramus, sweet youth and tall,
  And finds his trusty Thisby's mantle slain;
  Whereat, with blade, with bloody blameful blade,
  He bravely broach'd his boiling bloody breast,
  And Thisby, tarrying in mulberry shade,
  His dagger drew, and died. For all the rest,
  Let Lion, Moonshine, Wall, and Lovers twain,
  At large discourse, while here they do remain.
               Exit all but Wall.
THESEUS: I wonder if the Lion be to speak.
DEMETRIUS: No wonder, my Lord: one Lion may, when
  many asses do.
WALL: In this same Interlude, it doth befall,
  That I, one Snout (by name) present a wall:
  And such a wall, as I would have you think,
  That had in it a crannied hole or chink:

Through which the Lovers, Pyramus and Thisby,
Did whisper often, very secretly.
This loam, this rough-cast, and this stone doth show,
That I am that same Wall; the truth is so.
And this the cranny is, right and sinister,
Through which the fearful Lovers are to whisper.

THESEUS: Would you desire lime and hair to speak better?

DEMETRIUS: It is the wittiest partition, that ever I heard
discourse, my Lord.

THESEUS: Pyramus draws near the Wall, silence.

Enter Pyramus.

PYRAMUS: O grim-look'd night, O night with hue so
black,
O night, which ever art, when day is not:
O night, O night, alack, alack, alack,
I fear my Thisby's promise is forgot.
And thou O wall, O sweet, O lovely wall,
That stand'st between her father's ground and mine,
Thou wall, O wall, O sweet and lovely wall,
Show me thy chink, to blink through with mine eyne.
Thanks courteous wall. Jove shield thee well for this.
But what see I? No Thisby do I see.
O wicked wall, through whom I see no bliss,
Curs'd be thy stones for thus deceiving me.

THESEUS: The wall methinks being sensible, should curse
again.

PYRAMUS: No in truth sir, he should not. *Deceiving me*,
is Thisby's cue; she is to enter now, and I am to spy her
through the wall. You shall see it will fall pat as I told
you: yonder she comes.

Enter Thisbe.

THISBE: O wall, full often hast thou heard my moans,
For parting my fair Pyramus, and me.

My cherry lips have often kiss'd thy stones;
Thy stones with lime and hair knit up in thee.

PYRAMUS: I see a voice; now will I to the chink,
To spy and I can hear my Thisby's face.
Thisby?

THISBE: My Love thou art, my Love I think.

PYRAMUS: Think what thou wilt, I am thy Lover's grace,
And like Limander am I trusty still.

THISBE: And I like Helen till the Fates me kill.

PYRAMUS: Not Shafalus to Procrus, was so true.

THISBE: As Shafalus to Procrus, I to you.

PYRAMUS: O kiss me through the hole of this vile wall.

THISBE: I kiss the wall's hole, not your lips at all.

PYRAMUS: Wilt thou at Ninny's tomb meet me straightway?

THISBE: 'Tide life, 'tide death, I come without delay.

Exeunt Pyramus and Thisbe.

WALL: Thus have I Wall, my part discharged so;
And being done, thus Wall away doth go.

Exit.

THESEUS: Now is the Moon used between the two neighbours.

DEMETRIUS: No remedy my Lord, when walls are so
wilful, to hear without warning.

HIPPOLYTA: This is the silliest stuff that ever I heard.

THESEUS: The best in this kind are but shadows, and the
worst are no worse, if imagination amend them.

HIPPOLYTA: It must be your imagination then, and not
theirs.

THESEUS: If we imagine no worse of them than they of
themselves, they may pass for excellent men. Here come
two noble beasts in, a man and a Lion.

Enter Lion and Moonshine.

LION: You Ladies, you (whose gentle hearts do fear
 The smallest monstrous mouse that creeps on floor)
 May now perchance, both quake and tremble here,
 When Lion rough in wildest rage doth roar.
 Then know that I, one Snug the joiner am
 A Lion fell, nor else no Lion's dam:
 For if I should as Lion come in strife
 Into this place, 'twere pity on my life.

THESEUS: A very gentle beast, and of a good conscience.

DEMETRIUS: The very best at a beast, my Lord, that e'er
 I saw.

LYSANDER: This Lion is a very fox for his valour.

THESEUS: True, and a goose for his discretion.

DEMETRIUS: Not so my Lord: for his valour cannot carry
 his discretion, and the fox carries the goose.

THESEUS: His discretion I am sure cannot carry his valour:
 for the goose carries not the fox. It is well; leave it to his
 discretion, and let us listen to the Moon.

MOONSHINE: This lanthorn doth the horned Moon
 present.

DEMETRIUS: He should have worn the horns on his head.

THESEUS: He is no crescent, and his horns are invisible,
 within the circumference.

MOONSHINE: This lanthorn doth the horned Moon
 present:
 Myself the man i' th' Moon do seem to be.

THESEUS: This is the greatest error of all the rest; the man
 should be put into the lanthorn. How is it else the man i'
 th' Moon?

DEMETRIUS: He dares not come there for the candle. For
 you see, it is already in snuff.

HIPPOLYTA: I am aweary of this moon; would he would
 change.

THESEUS: It appears, by his small light of discretion, that he is in the wane: but yet in courtesy, in all reason, we must stay the time.

LYSANDER: Proceed Moon.

MOONSHINE: All that I have to say, is to tell you, that the lanthorn is the Moon; I, the man i' th' Moon; this thorn-bush, my thorn-bush; and this dog, my dog.

DEMETRIUS: Why all these should be in the lanthorn: for all these are in the Moon. But silence, here comes Thisbe.

Enter Thisbe.

THISBE: This is old Ninny's tomb. Where is my love?

LION: Oh.

The Lion roars, Thisbe runs off.

DEMETRIUS: Well roar'd Lion.

THESEUS: Well run Thisbe.

HIPPOLYTA: Well shone Moon.
Truly the Moon shines with a good grace.

Exit Lion.

THESEUS: Well moused Lion.

DEMETRIUS: And then came Pyramus.

LYSANDER: And so the Lion vanished.

Enter Pyramus.

PYRAMUS: Sweet Moon, I thank thee for thy sunny beams,
  I thank thee Moon, for shining now so bright;
  For by thy gracious, golden, glittering gleams,
  I trust to take of truest Thisby sight.
  But stay: O spite! but mark, poor Knight,
  What dreadful dole is here?
  Eyes do you see! how can it be!
  O dainty duck: O dear!
  Thy mantle good; what stain'd with blood!
  Approach ye Furies fell:

O Fates! come, come: cut thread and thrum,
Quail, crush, conclude, and quell.

THESEUS: This passion, and the death of a dear friend,
would go near to make a man look sad.

HIPPOLYTA: Beshrew my heart, but I pity the man.

PYRAMUS: O wherefore Nature, didst thou Lions frame?
Since Lion vile hath here deflower'd my dear:
Which is: no, no, which was the fairest Dame
That liv'd, that lov'd, that lik'd, that look'd with cheer
Come tears, confound: out sword, and wound
The pap of Pyramus:
Ay, that left pap, where heart doth hop;
Thus die I, thus, thus, thus.
Now am I dead, now am I fled, my soul is in the sky,
Tongue lose thy light, Moon take thy flight,

Exit Moonshine.

Now die, die, die, die, die.

Dies.

DEMETRIUS: No die, but an ace for him; for he is but one.

LYSANDER: Less than an ace man. For he is dead, he is
nothing.

THESEUS: With the help of a surgeon, he might yet
recover, and prove an ass.

HIPPOLYTA: How chance Moonshine is gone before?
Thisbe comes back, and finds her lover.

Enter Thisbe.

THESEUS: She will find him by starlight. Here she comes,
and her passion ends the play.

HIPPOLYTA: Methinks she should not use a long one for
such a Pyramus: I hope she will be brief.

DEMETRIUS: A mote will turn the balance, which Pyramus, which Thisbe is the better; he for a man, God
warrant us: she for a woman, God bless us.

LYSANDER: She hath spied him already, with those sweet eyes.

DEMETRIUS: And thus she means, *videlicet*.

THISBE: Asleep my Love? what, dead my dove?
O Pyramus arise:
Speak, speak. Quite dumb? Dead, dead? A tomb
Must cover thy sweet eyes.
These lily lips, this cherry nose,
These yellow cowslip cheeks,
Are gone, are gone: Lovers make moan:
His eyes were green as leeks.
O Sisters Three, come, come to me,
With hands as pale as milk,
Lay them in gore, since you have shore
With shears, his thread of silk.
Tongue not a word: come trusty sword:
Come blade, my breast imbrue:
And farewell friends, thus Thisbe ends;
Adieu, adieu, adieu.

THESEUS: Moonshine and Lion are left to bury the dead.

DEMETRIUS: Ay, and Wall too.

BOTTOM: No, I assure you, the wall is down that parted their fathers. Will it please you to see the Epilogue, or to hear a Bergomask dance, between two of our company?

THESEUS: No Epilogue, I pray you; for your play needs no excuse. Never excuse; for when the players are all dead, there need none to be blamed. Marry, if he that writ it had played Pyramus, and hang'd himself in Thisbe's garter, it would have been a fine Tragedy: and so it is truly, and very notably discharg'd. But come, your Bergomask: let your Epilogue alone.

A Bergomask dance.

The iron tongue of midnight hath told twelve.

Lovers to bed, 'tis almost fairy time.
I fear we shall out-sleep the coming morn,
As much as we this night have overwatch'd.
This palpable gross play hath well beguil'd
The heavy gait of night. Sweet friends to bed.
A fortnight hold we this solemnity,
In nightly revels; and new jollity.

Exeunt.

Enter Puck.

PUCK: Now the hungry lion roars,
And the wolf beholds the Moon:
Whilst the heavy ploughman snores,
All with weary task fordone.
Now the wasted brands do glow,
Whilst the screech-owl, screeching loud,
Puts the wretch that lies in woe,
In remembrance of a shroud.
Now it is the time of night,
That the graves, all gaping wide,
Every one lets forth his sprite,
In the church-way paths to glide.
And we Fairies, that do run,
By the triple Hecate's team,
From the presence of the Sun,
Following darkness like a dream,
Now are frolic; not a mouse
Shall disturb this hallow'd house.
I am sent with broom before,
To sweep the dust behind the door.
Enter the King and Queen of Fairies with their train.
OBERON: Through the house give glimmering light,
By the dead and drowsy fire,

Every elf and fairy sprite,
Hop as light as bird from brier,
And this ditty after me,
Sing and dance it trippingly.

TITANIA: First rehearse your song by rote,
To each word a warbling note.
Hand in hand, with fairy grace,
Will we sing and bless this place.

The Song.

OBERON: *Now until the break of day,*
Through this house each Fairy stray.
To the best bride-bed will we,
Which by us shall blessed be:
And the issue there create,
Ever shall be fortunate:
So shall all the couples three,
Ever true in loving be:
And the blots of Nature's hand,
Shall not in their issue stand.
Never mole, hare lip, nor scar,
Nor mark prodigious, such as are
Despised in nativity,
Shall upon their children be.
With this field-dew consecrate,
Every Fairy take his gait,
And each several chamber bless,
Through this Palace with sweet peace,
Ever shall in safety rest,
And the owner of it blest.
Trip away, make no stay;
Meet me all by break of day.

Exeunt all but Puck.

PUCK: If we shadows have offended,
Think but this (and all is mended)
That you have but slumber'd here,
While these visions did appear.
And this weak and idle theme,
No more yielding but a dream,
Gentles, do not reprehend.
If you pardon, we will mend.
And as I am an honest Puck,
If we have unearned luck,
Now to scape the serpent's tongue,
We will make amends ere long:
Else the Puck a liar call.
So good night unto you all.
Give me your hands, if we be friends,
And Robin shall restore amends.

Exit.

NOTES

References are to the page and line of this edition;
there are lines 33 to the full page.

The Actors' Names, *Hippolyta, Queen of the Amazons*:
They were a legendary race of female warriors who
lived in South Russia; Theseus had defeated them in
battle.

Long withering out: i.e. by refusing to die.   **P. 21 L. 8**

pale companion: melancholy fellow.   **P. 21 L. 19**

Stand forth Demetrius . . . Stand forth Lysander. In the   **P. 21 L. 30**
Quartos and Folio these words are stage directions.   **P. 22 L. 3**
Modern editors incorporate them into Egeus'
speech.

rhymes: i.e. love spells.   **P. 22 L. 6**

stolen . . . fantasy: made a false impression on her   **P. 22 L. 10**
imagination.

conceits: pretty devices.   **P. 22 L. 11**

your father should be as a god. This theory of the   **P. 22 L. 25**
relation of child to father was very generally
accepted, especially by old-fashioned parents. So
Mildred the good daughter in *Eastward Ho* (1605)
when her father produces Touchstone as her future
husband, replies: 'Sir, I am all yours; your body
gave me life, your care and love, happiness of life;
let your virtue still direct it, for to your wisdom I
wholly dispose myself.'

this kind: i.e. care of marriage.   **P. 22 L. 33**

my virgin patent: the privilege of my virginity.   **P. 23 L. 26**

sealing-day: day of formal agreement.   **P. 23 L. 30**

fit your fancies: make your love agree.   **P. 24 L. 31**

in a spleen: in a flash of temper.   **P. 25 L. 28**

with the golden head: Cupid's arrows causing love are   **P. 26 L. 21**
headed with gold.

the Carthage Queen: Aeneas, on his escape from the   **P. 26 L. 24** sack of Troy, came to Carthage, where Dido, the Queen, fell in love with him. Aeneas deserted Dido, whereupon she mounted on a funeral pyre and killed herself in the flames.

P. 27 L. 5   *favour:* with the double meaning of 'beauty' and 'love'.

P. 27 L. 30   *Phoebe:* i.e. Diana the moon.

P. 28 L. 7   *stranger companies:* the emendation usually accepted for the texts' 'strange companions'.

P. 29 L. 6   *dear expense:* bitter bargain.

P. 29 L. 15   *generally:* Bottom, who usually gets the long words wrong, means *severally:* separately.

P. 30 L. 6   *my chief humour is for a tyrant.* It seems likely that in the person of Bully Bottom Shakespeare is parodying Edward Alleyne, the great tragedian and leader of the rival company, the Admiral's Men. Alleyne was particularly famous for furious and tyrannical parts. He made his name as Tamburlane (Marlowe's ranting conqueror), Dr Faustus, Hieronimo in the *Spanish Tragedy*, Barabas in the *Jew of Malta,* and Orlando Furioso.

P. 30 L. 7   *Ercles . . . make all split:* Ercles (or Hercules) on the stage was a furious character. Hamlet is a severe critic of this kind of acting. 'It offends me to the soul to hear a robustious periwig-pated fellow tear a passion to tatters, to the very rags, to split the ears of the groundlings.' 'To tear a cat' is a proverbial expression for this style of acting; but our ancestors did such revolting things to cats that it may have had an origin in fact.

P. 30 L. 23   *Thisne, Thisne:* either Bottom is mincingly pronouncing Thisby's name in a monstrous little voice, or, as some editors suggest, the word is *thissen:* 'like this 'ere', in this way.

P. 31 L. 13   *Duchess and the Ladies:* See Introduction p. 15.

P. 31 L. 18   *aggravate:* Bottom's version of 'moderate'.

P. 31 L. 23   *gentleman-like man:* this compliment, above all others, fetches Bottom.

P. 31 L. 29   *purple in grain beard.* A whole book could be written on beards, which at this time were universally worn, cut to symbolize the wearer's character, and sometimes dyed. This is still the custom in some parts of India, particularly the North. My Indian bearer, whose beard was grey, would sometimes make the most astonishing improvements on nature from carrot colour, through scarlet to purple.

French . . . no hair: the result of the French disease. P. 31 L. 32

by moonlight: The behaviour of the moon is arbitrary. P. 32 L. 3 At the opening of the play it is four days from new moon; the events of the night take place in full moonlight; but these (from Act II to the awakening of the lovers and the return of Bottom at the end of Act IV) are all part of the Dream.

obscenely: probably for 'obscurely'. P.32 L. 9

hold or cut bow-strings: The phrase has not been satis- P. 32 L. 12 factorily explained. It means, presumably, 'come what may'.

cowslips . . . pensioners be. The littleness of the P. 33 L. 25 fairies is constantly emphasized. Queen Elizabeth's Gentlemen Pensioners, her personal bodyguard, were chosen for their size and comeliness from gentlemen of good family.

changeling: usually, an ugly child left by the fairies P. 33 L. 7 who exchanged it for a beautiful child which they stole. Titania's Indian boy is the stolen, not the exchanged child.

Robin Goodfellow. In the Quarto the speech headings P. 33 L. 18 are sometimes 'Puck' and sometimes 'Robin'. The popular belief about Robin Goodfellow can be seen in Nashe's *Terrors of the Night,* 1593. 'In the time of infidelity, when spirits were so familiar with men that they called them *Dii Penates,* their household Gods or their Lares, they never sacrificed unto them till Sun-setting. The Robin-good-fellows, Elves, Fairies, Hobgoblins of our latter age, which idolatrous former days and the fantastical world of Greece yclept *Fawns, Satyrs, Dryads,* and *Hamadryads,* did most of their merry pranks in the Night.

Then ground they malt, and had hempen shirts for
their labours, danced in rounds in green meadows,
pinched maids in their sleep that swept not their
houses clean, and led poor Travellers out of their
way notoriously.' . . . '*In diebus illis* when *Corineus*
and *Gogmagog* were little boys, I will not gainsay
that he was wont to jest and sport with country
people, and play the good fellow amongst kitchen
wenches, sitting in an evening by the fire side making
of possets, and come a-wooing to them in the likeness
of a cooper, or a curmudgeonly purchaser: and
sometimes he would dress himself like a Barber, and
wash and shave all those that lay in such a chamber:
otherwhile like a stale cutter of Queenhithe, he
would justle men in their own houses, pluck
them out of bed by the heels, and dance in chains
from one chamber to another.' (Edited by R. B.
McKerrow, i. 347 and 167.)

P. 34 L. 6   *And tailor cries.* No one has yet explained why she
should cry 'tailor', unless perchance it was a tailor
in the party who cried and coughed. There may be a
topical jest here, alluding to some old aunt, who had
misfortunes similar to those of Mrs Mascall, the
tripe-wife, which were amusing Londoners in the
first weeks of 1595. The tripe-wife was a widow with
some property, which various suitors sought by way
of marriage. First they tried to cheat her with the aid
of Judith Phillips (alias Doll Pope), a wise woman.
Judith flattered the old woman with various lies and
so obtained possession of some of her jewellery and
trinkets. 'She also told the widow that she must have
a turkey and a capon to give to the Queen of the
Fairies, which the widow provided.' Mrs Mascall
however soon discovered that she had been cheated
and Judith was arrested. A few days later one of the
suitors was successful. With the aid of her sister, he
inveigled her into a drinking party, and when she
was drunk drew a promise of marriage from her.
'Shortly after, the widow sitting asleep by the fire,
he valiantly coming behind her, pulled the stool

from her, when down fell she, and he by (or upon)
her, with that learned and witty adverb in his mouth
"Keep the widow waking!"' Before she had re-
covered her senses, she was hurried before a priest
and married. (*Second Elizabethan Journal*, pp. 5, 18.)

cough: In the Quarto the spelling is 'coffe' and   P. 34 L. 6
'loffe'.

Corin . . . Phillida: typical names of shepherd and   P. 34 L. 22
shepherdess in pastoral poetry.

buskin'd: wearing buskins, i.e. hunting boots.   P. 34 L. 27

Perigenia . . . Aegles . . . Ariadne . . . Antiopa. All these   P. 35 L. 1
names come from the life of Theseus as given in
North's translation of Plutarch's *Lives*.

beached margent: the margin of pebbles.   P. 35 L. 8

Therefore the winds . . . : See Introduction p. 15.   P. 35 L. 11

nine men's morris: 'Merels was a game for two players   P. 35 L. 21
or parties, each of whom had the same number of
pebbles, disks, pegs, or pins. It was also known as
Nine Men's Morris, Fivepenny Morris, and Three
Men's Morris, according to the number of "men"
used. The usual form of the diagram on which it is
played is a square with one or more squares inside it.
The pegs or stones placed at set points are moved by
one side so as to take up the men of the other.
Cotgrave speaks of "the boyish game called Merilles,
or five-penny Morris" as being "played here most
commonly with stones, but in France with pawns,
or men made of purpose, and termed Merelles".
Various local varieties have been described by
antiquarian writers. In the open air form of the
game the squares are made in the turf with knives.'
(*Shakespeare's England*, ii. 467.)

want their winter here. Editors finding no sense in   P. 35 L. 24
'here' emend variously: probably 'cheer' is the best
guess, the Quarto spelling being 'heere'.

a mermaid . . . fancy-free: This passage is usually taken   P. 37 L. 10
as a reference to Queen Elizabeth (the Virgin Queen
whose bosom was impenetrable to the arrows of
Love) and some entertainment at a great house at

which a mermaid was presented on a dolphin. Such shows were notable, as at the famous Kenilworth Revels in 1575, and more recently at Elvetham in 1591.

P. 37 L. 29 *love-in-idleness*: a name for the pansy.

P. 38 L. 16 *I am invisible.* This piece of information for the benefit of the audience is crude, but probably some cloak or robe was put on to show Oberon's invisibility. In the papers of Philip Henslowe who owned the Rose Theatre, there is a note that in 1598 he spent £3 10s. for the Admiral's Men for 'a robe for to goo invisibell' and 'a gown for Nembia'. (*Henslowe Papers,* ed. W. W. Greg, p. 123.) Wordsworth perhaps gives the clue to the peculiarity of the robe. In Book VII of *The Prelude* he describes the shows visited in London, such as:

> The champion, Jack the Giant-killer; Lo!
> He dons his coat of darkness: on the stage
> Walks, and achieves his wonders, from the eye
> Of living Mortal covert, 'as the moon
> Hid in her vacant interlunar cave'.
> Delusion bold! and how can it be wrought?
> The garb he wears is black as death, the word
> *'Invisible'* flames forth upon his chest.

P. 38 L. 21 *slay . . . slayeth*: the usually accepted emendation for 'stay', 'stayeth'.

P. 39 L. 3 *spaniel*: Shakespeare often used the spaniel as the type of fawning dog.

P 39 L. 29 *Apollo . . . Daphne*: Apollo hotly pursued the chaste Daphne who was saved by being transformed into a laurel bush. Helena says that the natural order is reversed: the modest maid is the pursuer.

P. 39 L. 30 *griffin*: a fearful fowl, part eagle, part lion.

P. 40 L. 19 *oxlips*: in appearance a cross between a primrose and a cowslip.

P. 44 L. 24 *transparent*: i.e. because her heart is visible.

P. 47 L. 7 *eight and six*: the common ballad metre of eight syllables followed by six.

a Lion among Ladies: See Introduction p. 15.   P. 47 L. 13

hempen home-spuns: i.e. simpletons dressed in their home-woven clothes.   P. 48 L. 25

cues and all: the actor's part was (and still is) written out with the last few words of the previous speaker's part as cue.   P. 49 L. 18

Cobweb . . . finger: The primitive method of stopping the blood from a cut finger was to clap a cobweb on the wound.   P. 52 L. 11

Squash . . . Peascod: the squash is the unripe pod before it becomes the peascod.   P. 52 L. 14

russet-pated choughs: grey-headed jackdaws.   P. 53 L. 24

earth . . . Antipodes: i.e. the moon will pass through the earth and appear at the other side, to the annoyance of the sun.   P. 54 L. 26

mispris'd mood: mistaken emotion.   P. 55 L. 16

debt . . . owe: i.e. a man in sorrow cannot sleep; sleep's debt to sorrow thus grows heavier.   P. 55 L. 28

sighs . . . blood: sighs were supposed to consume the heart's blood.   P. 56 L. 8

Two of the first . . . one crest. After marriage the coats of arms of husband and wife are united in one coat under one crest.   P. 60 L. 2

seem to break loose . . . : This is the Folio reading. Hermia is clutching Lysander. Demetrius taunts him, saying that he pretends to want a fight, but in reality is ready enough to be held back by a woman.   P. 61 L. 16

knot-grass: knotgrass was believed to stunt growth. As gardeners know, it is a clinging pest, difficult to eradicate.   P. 63 L. 32

crossways . . . have burial: suicides used to be buried at cross roads.   P. 65 L. 26

spirits of another sort: i.e. not infernal spirits of darkness.   P. 65 L. 31

They sleep all the act: i.e. they remain in their places during the interval.   P. 68 L. 23

P. 70 L. 6   *woodbine:* Shakespeare only uses woodbine twice: in this play (p. 40, l. 20) and in *Much Ado* where Beatrice is couched in 'woodbine cover'; it usually means 'honeysuckle'. He may however be using the other meaning of 'bindweed'—convolvulus.

P. 70 L. 7   *female ivy:* because the ivy is said to be 'married' to the elm, to which it clings.

P. 71 L. 16   *these five:* i.e. the four lovers and Bottom.

P. 72 L. 12   *observation is perform'd:* i.e. 'the rite of May' (see p. 73, l. 9).

P. 72 L. 31   *match'd . . . bells:* In Elizabethan times a pack of hounds was not of uniform breed but so chosen that their cry made a musical harmony. When King James I first came to England in 1603 'from Stamford Hill to London was made a train with a tame deer, with such twinings and doubles, that the hounds could not take it faster than his Majesty proceeded; yet still, by the industry of the huntsman, and the subtlety of him that made the train in a full-mouthed cry all the way, never farther distant than one close from the highway, whereby his Majesty rid, and for the most part directly against his Majesty, whom, together with the whole company, had the lee wind from the hounds, to the end they might the better perceive and judge of the uniformity in the cries'. (Nichols' *Progresses of King James I*, i. 139.)

P. 73 L. 17   *Saint Valentine:* birds were supposed to mate on St. Valentine's Day (14th February).

P. 75 L. 28   *patch'd fool:* i.e. a fool in his particoloured motley coat.

P. 75 L. 33   *ballad of this dream:* printers and ballad-mongers did a good trade by producing a doggerel ballad hot upon any extraordinary event. Ballads were hawked and sung to one of several popular tunes.

P. 76 L. 3   *her death:* i.e. Thisbe's.

P. 76 L. 26   *sixpence a day, during his life:* Grateful patrons sometimes awarded their entertainers in this way. Thus

Will Kemp, at this time Clown of the Lord Chamberlain's Company, after his dance to Norwich in 1600 was awarded 40/- yearly during his life by the Mayor of Norwich.

The Lunatic . . . Poet: See Introduction p. 16.   P. 77 L. 29

brow of Egypt: i.e. a dark skin; 'Egyptians' were   P. 78 L. 2
gypsies.

But all the story . . . great constancy: i.e. 'but their story,   P. 78 L. 14
and the fact that they all agree shows that it is more
than imagination and appears consistent.'

Call Philostrate: There is a notable change in the   P. 78 L. 32
Folio here; it omits Philostrate from this scene and
substitutes Egeus as master of ceremonies. The
Quarto makes Theseus read out for himself the list
of entertainments. The Folio improves on this by
splitting up the catalogue and comments between
Theseus and Lysander: an arrangement which I have
preferred to follow.

The thrice three Muses . . . beggary: This is apparently   P. 79 l 15
a topical allusion, variously interpreted. If it was
written in 1594-5, then it refers to the sensational
death in poverty of Robert Greene in September,
1592. Greene's death was still being talked and
written about, and in 1594 one R.B. produced
Greene's Funerals. If it was added later, then it
echoes the common complaint of satirists from 1597
onwards that learned men are neglected.

wondrous strange snow. Editors, not content with the   P. 79 L. 23
epithet 'strange' emend to taste – 'seething',
'swarthy', 'sable', 'flaming', 'swart', etc.

wretchedness . . . perishing: i.e. humble folk ruining   P. 80 L. 21
themselves through excess of zeal.

noble respect . . . not merit: i.e. a noble mind accepts   P. 80 L. 27
the good intention for the bad performance.

great clerks: learned scholars. Queen Elizabeth had   P. 80 L. 29
often to endure long orations whenever she went on
progress. Her visit to Oxford in 1592 was fairly
recent when the play was written. Various academic

exercises were performed before her. At one of these 'stood up one Mr Sydney (who was placed in the lowest form) being thereunto required by the Proctors. He forgat his congés, used no speech at all to Her Majesty, but dealt with the answerer as though Her Majesty had not been there' (Nichol's *Progresses of Queen Elizabeth*). The general complaint however was that the Oxford scholars once on their feet could not stop.

P. 81 L. 15   *If we offend:* Quince by mistaking his punctuation makes woeful sense of his words.

P. 81 L. 25   *upon points:* punctuation marks.

P. 81 L. 32   The Folio inserts, after 'who is next', the separate stage direction *Tawyer with a Trumpet before them*.

P. 82 L. 20   *bloody blameful blade:* This excessive alliteration, much loved by earlier poets, was now out of fashion.

P. 82 L. 21   *broach'd:* in the sense of tapping a cask.

P. 83 L. 5   *sinister:* accented siníster, with the double meaning of 'ominous' and 'left hand'.

P. 84 L. 8   *Limander ... Helen ... Shafalus ... Procrus:* he means Leander and Hero, Cephalus and Procris, whose stories were well known to this well-bred audience.

P. 84 L. 21   *Moon used:* the Folio reads 'moral down'. Most editors accept the emendation 'mural down', or 'mure all down'.

P. 85 L. 31   *in snuff:* smoking. Before self-consuming wicks were invented for candles, the wick needed to be periodically snuffed, or it emitted a foul smoke.

P. 86 L. 19   *moused:* i.e. as a cat tosses and tears a mouse.

P. 87 L. 1   *cut ... thrum:* The thrum is the end of thread in weaving. So the phrase means 'ruin everything'.

P. 87 L. 8   *Which is: no, no, which* was *the fairest Dame:* See note on p. 30, l. 6. This seems to be another parody of the histrionic style of the great Alleyne. One of his greatest triumphs was in Hieronymo's lamentations over his son Horatio:

Alas, it is Horatio, my sweet son.
O no, but he that whilom *was* my son.

O was it thou that call'dst me from my bed?
O speak, if any spark of life remain.
I am thy Father; who hath slain my son?
What savage monster, not of human kind,
Hath here been glutted with thy harmless blood,
And left thy bloody corpse dishonoured here,
For me amidst these dark and deathful shades,
To drown thee with an ocean of my tears?
O heavens, why made you night to cover sin?
By day this deed of darkness had not been.
O earth, why didst thou not in time devour
The vile prophaner of this sacred bower?
O poor Horatio, what hadst thou misdone,
To lose thy life ere life was new begun?
O wicked butcher, what so ere thou wert,
How could thou strangle virtue and desert?
Ay me most wretched, that have lost my joy,
In losing my Horatio, my sweet boy.

And:

O eyes, no eyes, but fountains fraught with tears;
O life, no life, but lively form of death;
O world, no world, but mass of public wrongs,
Confused and filled with murder and misdeeds.

Pyramus' dying speech is not more ridiculous than
other dying speeches in the plays of the Admiral's
Men. Thus Stukeley in *The Battle of Alcazar,* when
fatally stabbed, turns to the audience with:

Thus Stukeley slain with many a deadly stab,
Dies in these desert fields of Africa.
Hark friends, and with the story of my life
Let me beguile the torment of my death.

Hereupon he gives 42 lines of autobiography and
ends:

Now go, and in that bed of honour die
Where brave Sebastian's breathless corse doth lie.
Here endeth Fortune, rule, and bitter rage:
Here ends Tom Stukeley's pilgrimage. *He dieth.*

Bergomask dance: a fantastic rustic dance.

P. 89 L. 23   *triple Hecate:* the goddess Diana was called three-formed because she was worshipped as Diana on earth, as Cynthia, Phoebe (or Luna) in the sky, and as Proserpine (or Hecate) in the underworld.

P. 91 L. 11   *serpent's tongue:* i.e. hissing.

P. 91 L. 15   *Give me your hands:* Give me a clap.

GLOSSARY

abridgement : pastime.
aby : pay for.
Acheron : a river in Hades.
adamant : magnet, lodestone.
admirable : astonishing.
against : in anticipation of.
argument : plot of a story.
artificial : creative.

barm : yeast.
bated : excepted.
bay'd : brought to bay.
beshrew : bad luck to.
beteem : cause to bring forth, allow.
bootless : in vain.
bottle : bundle.
brake : bush, thicket.
brief : synopsis.
by'r Lakin : by Our Lady.

cankers : maggots.
canker-blossom : destructive maggot.
capacity : understanding.
centre : i.e. of the earth.
childing : fertile.
coil : stir.
collied : blackened.
composed : formed, created.
con : learn by heart.
continents : bonds, that which contains.
coy : caress.
crab : crab-apple.
crannied : cracked.

crazed : cracked.
cross : impediment.
curst : shrewish.

darkling : in the dark.
defect : for 'effect'.
derived : descended.
dewberries : a kind of blackberries.

eglantine : sweetbriar.
enamelled : painted.
erewhile : a short while ago.
exposition : for 'disposition'.
eyne : eyes.

fancy : (1) love (2) imagination.
feigning : deceptive.
flew'd : with large cheeks.
fond : foolish.

gaud : gawdy trifle.
gleek : make sarcastic remarks.

henchman : servant.
Hiems : winter.

impeach : discredit.
interlude : play.

jole : check.
juvenal : youth.

Lakin : Our Lady.
latch'd : caught, enchanted.
leviathan : whale.

lob : lubber, clown.
lodestar : guiding star.

margent : margin.
mazed : bewildered.
mechanicals : workmen.
mewed : caged.
mimic : actor.
minimus : littlest thing.
misgraffed : ill-grafted.
misprision : mistakes.
mote : speck of dust.
murrion : plague stricken.

neaf : fist.
neeze : sneeze.
nole : head.

oes : circles.
ounce : lynx.
owe : own.

palpable-gross : excessively crude.
passing : exceedingly.
patches : clowns.
pelting : paltry.
periods : full stops.
Philomel : the nightingale.
Phœbe : the moon.
plainsong : simple melody.
point : limit.
presently : immediately.

quantity : proportion.
quern : hand mill.

recorder : a woodwind instrument.
repair : return.
reremice : bats.
respect : estimation.
roundel : round dance.

sanded : sand coloured.
scrip : writing, scroll.
sphery : star-like.
square : squabble.
steppe : steep.
still : always.
streak : stroke.
surfeit : excess.

thorough : through.
tiring-house : dressing-room.
toys : trifles.
trace : track.
traders : trading vessels.

unbreathed : unexercised.

vantage : superiority.
vaward : vanguard.

weed : garment.
wode : mad.
woosell : blackbird.
wot : know.

PENGUIN POPULAR CLASSICS

Published or forthcoming

Aesop	Aesop's Fables
Hans Andersen	Fairy Tales
Louisa May Alcott	Good Wives
	Little Women
Eleanor Atkinson	Greyfriars Bobby
Jane Austen	Emma
	Mansfield Park
	Northanger Abbey
	Persuasion
	Pride and Prejudice
	Sense and Sensibility
R. M. Ballantyne	The Coral Island
J. M. Barrie	Peter Pan
R. D. Blackmore	Lorna Doone
Anne Brontë	Agnes Grey
	The Tenant of Wildfell Hall
Charlotte Brontë	Jane Eyre
	The Professor
	Shirley
	Villette
Emily Brontë	Wuthering Heights
John Buchan	The Thirty-Nine Steps
Frances Hodgson Burnett	A Little Princess
	The Secret Garden
Samuel Butler	The Way of All Flesh
Lewis Carroll	Alice's Adventures in Wonderland
	Through the Looking Glass
Geoffrey Chaucer	The Canterbury Tales
G. K. Chesterton	Father Brown Stories
Erskine Childers	The Riddle of the Sands
John Cleland	Fanny Hill
Wilkie Collins	The Moonstone
	The Woman in White
Sir Arthur Conan Doyle	The Adventures of Sherlock Holmes
	The Hound of the Baskervilles
	A Study in Scarlet

PENGUIN POPULAR CLASSICS

Published or forthcoming

PENGUIN POPULAR CLASSICS

Published or forthcoming

PENGUIN POPULAR CLASSICS

PENGUIN POPULAR POETRY

Published or forthcoming

The Selected Poems *of:*

Matthew Arnold
William Blake
Robert Browning
Robert Burns
Lord Byron
John Donne
Thomas Hardy
John Keats
Rudyard Kipling
Alexander Pope
Alfred Tennyson
Walt Whitman
William Wordsworth
William Yeats

and collections of:

Sixteenth-Century Poetry
Seventeenth-Century Poetry
Eighteenth-Century Poetry
Poetry of the Romantics
Victorian Poetry
Twentieth-Century Poetry